USE JAPANESE AT HOME

Way Usable Japanese for Families

Second Edition

Written by Adelaide Olguin

made with love by
TALKBOX.MOM
Talk in a foreign language with your family!

© 2024, 2017 by Adelaide Olguin

All rights reserved. No part of this book may be reproduced in any form or by any means without prior permission in writing from the publisher, TalkBox.Mom, Inc.

TalkBox.Mom books and programs are available for quantity discounts and fundraising opportunities when being used by families of students at a language immersion school or families in a home school group.
Go to www.talkbox.mom/groups for more information.

To the greatest language teachers in the world— mothers.

YOUR HOME IS A
POWERFUL PLACE.

IT'S WHERE YOU
LEARNED YOUR
FIRST LANGUAGE.

IT'S WHERE YOU
TAUGHT YOUR CHILD
THEIR FIRST LANGUAGE.

AND IT'S WHERE,
YOUR FAMILY
CAN LEARN THEIR
SECOND OR THIRD.

OPENING CREDITS

Thank you to the incredible women who ensured you'll talk like they do with their families in their native language and not like you walked out of a dusty, old textbook.

Yumiko Koganezawa	Ai Sato
Yuko Wylie	Sachi Nasu
Hiromi Kawaragi	Ayaka Hosokawa

Our goal was for you to sound like native speaking mothers, fathers, and children—not foreigners who walked out of a language class, whose word or sentence choices seem disconnected and super formal.

We never used old, outdated words, so you won't sound like an old textbook or someone's grandpa. We used words families are actually using.

We avoided having direct translations for this same reason. We didn't want you to simply say a phrase in Japanese that you say in English.

We wanted these phrases to be what a Japanese speaking parent or child would actually say in a specific situation. Sometimes, it's the same kind of thing. Sometimes it's different.

In any case, you'll sound convincing.

Table of Contents

Audio Companion	9
Hello! Of Course.	11
My Story	13
How to Guide	17
You're Invited!	31
What the Banner?	35
A	37
B	41
C	71
D	87
E	109
F	115
G	123
H	133
I	143
J	145
K	147
L	151

M	163
N	171
O	177
P	183
Q	195
R	197
S	201
T	231
U	245
V	249
W	251
Y	265
Z	267
Helping Children Reply Back	269
Getting Outside Your Comfort Zone	273
Your Toolbox	279
Goodbye	281
Index - *look up words here*	283

There is native speaker audio for every single phrase in this book, plus a system to help you track your progress as you listen, practice, and use your phrases in the **TalkBox.Mom Companion App.**

At the time of your purchase, you received non-transferable app access directly tied to your email address. If you don't already have access to the audio from the time of your purchase, please email your receipt to support@talkbox.mom so we can get you set up in the app.

To download the TalkBox.Mom Companion App on your phone, search for "TalkBox.Mom Companion App" inside your phone's app store (Android or Apple). After downloading the app, log in with your username and password. You can reset your password using your email address on the login page if you have no idea what your password is.

If you have any other problems or questions, please email support. Our team would love to help you!

♡ support@talkbox.mom

Hello! Of Course.

Many people think that learning a language starts with colors, numbers, and the ABCs. But that's what our kids do in preschool after they can already speak the language.

This is not where language learning begins. And starting with the ABCs and colors is definitely not language immersion or the path to fluency.

> There is hardly another civilised nation so dull in acquiring foreign tongues as we English of the present time; but, probably, **the fault lies rather in the way we set about the study** than in any natural incapacity for languages."
> - Charlotte Mason[1]

Learning to use a language looks like starting your day off, greeting each other, and eating in that language. It looks like grocery shopping in that language while helping each other or sometimes hearing kids complain. If your extended family speaks that language, it looks like using that language at family events. If your family doesn't, it looks like telling your child to go back, flush the toilet, and wash their hands in your "secret language." ☺ Everyone else will be impressed by your language skills—not knowing how gross your child is being.

> At TalkBox.Mom, we help families, like yours, start talking in a foreign language the exact same day they start. You don't wait to talk until year two or year... well, never. You talk from day one.

We can help your family start talking right away because we copy the approach of the best language teachers in the world: parents.

Yes, parents. Think about it. Who taught your kids to talk before they ever learned grammar and reading? You did.

As moms and dads, we teach babies and toddlers all over the world to talk at a native level—the most coveted level of learning a language. We have a higher success rate of teaching languages than high schools, colleges, and universities.

With TalkBox.Mom, we give you the tools to learn and teach another language using our proven roadmap and various fluency approaches based on natural language progression. We also help you lean into the skills you already have to teach a language successfully as a parent.

Plus, everything in our language programs are made by native-speaking women who want you to sound like you're from their country—not like you walked out of an outdated textbook.

And, yes, there is audio for every single phrase in our program. We mean it when we say that we'll give you all the tools to make learning another language feel easy, fun, doable, and the biggest confidence boost you've ever gotten.

And now, with your family, you get to use a language with this phrasebook and hear it for yourself!

My Story

Before I read the words of Charlotte Mason and M. Gouin, I too realized that "the classical method, with its grammar, its dictionary, and its translations, is a delusion."[2]

You see, my husband and I put everything in storage to travel around the world with our two boys to play and explore outside. We started in Brazil, and I had a verb conjugation book, a college textbook, vocabulary cards, and two little boys to learn Portuguese with!

I had tried learning other languages this same way (well, minus the little boys)—only to leave me feeling anxious whenever I went to speak. But this is how learning a language is done, right? 😣

When I announced to my three-year-old that we needed to learn to conjugate a verb before going outside, he stared at me like I was out of my mind and said, "We didn't come to Brazil to sit in a room."

And I realized that he said this wise statement without ever learning to conjugate verbs or without ever looking at flashcards. As someone who studied philosophy and languages at the University, I was self-aware enough to realize that I had been sucked into a very flawed but widespread model of language learning. It hit me that parents teach languages so much faster and before their kids can read—without grammar and vocab worksheets.

So I decided that I was going to teach a language like a mom and learn like a child with my family. Within two weeks, I was shocked when we were talking in and understanding Portuguese with native speakers in Brazil. Absolutely shocked. And as the months rolled on, we kept talking and understanding more and more.

From country to country, I continued to develop and optimize this approach as we traveled for two years. Each time we learned faster and were reaching our goal: really speaking the language! Queue a whole ton of fireworks!

But this wasn't enough. I knew any family could learn a language this way. Not just mine. I could feel it in my heart. You specifically were in my heart. Your hopes, your dreams of being able to use another language with your family. Before I ever met you here, I was thinking about you and knew I needed to do this for you.

So I created TalkBox.Mom with an amazing team of women to give you life-changing results.

I know that when you and your family can actually use a language, you can change your future work and educational opportunities. You can help others in your community. You can connect with family. You can make real connections as you travel. You can truly become a global citizen.

If you don't have your first box to use with this phrasebook, go to **www.talkbox.mom/japanese**! Then please introduce yourself in our private accountability group. You'll get a private invitation exclusively for families in our signature program:
The TalkBox.Mom Boxes.

I'd love to know what led you to want to learn Japanese with your family.

I want to meet you! I want to hear your progress and see you reach your daily goals. After all, I made TalkBox.Mom for you.

See you there!

xo

Adelaide Olguin

How to Guide

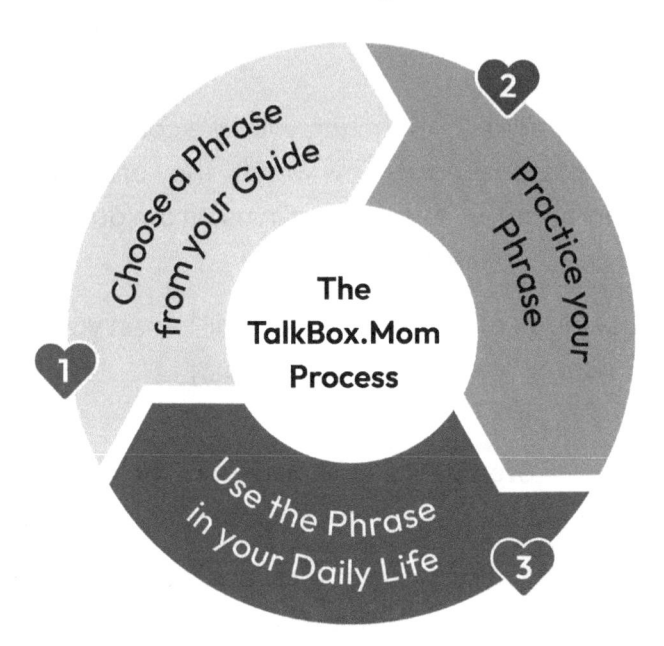

The TalkBox.Mom Process

1. Choose a Phrase from your Guide
2. Practice your Phrase
3. Use the Phrase in your Daily Life

The TalkBox.Mom Process has three completely doable steps to get your family talking.

First, you pick your 1-5 Focus Phrases. Yes, full phrases—not individual words or verb conjugations.

> But one verb is nothing; you want the child to learn [Japanese]..." - *Charlotte Mason*[3]

We recommend picking the bulk of your phrases from the boxes and one phrase every couple of days from the phrasebook or other guides like the Homeschool Phrases.

Second, you'll practice the phrases. It's very important to practice your phrases so your children are ready to use them in real life, which brings us to our next step!

Third, you'll use those phrases in real life. The goal is to add the phrases to your everyday life!

By following the TalkBox.Mom Process, you'll be learning to use full sentences with your family and continue to use those phrases in your life.

> Of course, his teacher, will take care... that as he learns new words, they are put into sentences and kept in use from day to day." - *Charlotte Mason*[4]

Here's a closer look at how these steps will look in your day with your family as well as some things to avoid!

Step 1: Pick 1-5 Focus Phrases
🕐 Time Needed: typically 30 seconds to 2 minutes

The first step is to choose only one to five Focus Phrases. This step is actually really hard for many people because it's so tempting to want to start with, well, everything! However, I promise that you'll learn everything much faster if you focus on one to five phrases.

Why? By focusing on a small number of phrases, you'll learn those phrases faster and deeper than if you spread yourself too thin. You'll also be able to give the phrases the attention they need to be practiced and used in real life. It's much more doable to implement two phrases with your child than 20 in a single day.

> That they should learn a few—two or three, four or five—new [Japanese] words daily...." - *Charlotte Mason*[5]

Even if it feels "too light" for you as the parent, the goal isn't that you're learning a whole bunch of things. It's that you're using the language. Using the language requires a deep and narrow focus that consistently grows.

This small focus helps lay a strong foundation. As these phrases are really internalized when they are practiced and used, they start to feel like second nature (aka a second language).

When this happens, the following sets of phrases you work on continue to become even easier, especially if you start your first box in the TalkBox.Mom program because it's designed to help you make exponential progress.

So please allow yourself to learn everything faster by focusing on one to five phrases—not by focusing on everything all at once.

> To start, have your child color in the heart of one phrase in this guide.

I recommend starting with just one phrase your first day so you can take the phrases through the entire TalkBox.Mom Process.

If you have the first box, start with the first phrase on your Challenge Checklist, and then in your second Practice Session add one phrase from this phrasebook.

As you work through this phrasebook, pick Focus Phrases that:

#1. You NEED to say.
#2. You WANT to say.
#3. You say ALL THE TIME.

Do not start at the beginning of this book by learning phrases from A-Z. You'll make faster progress if you focus on choosing phrases that have your family's specific needs and wants—not by learning every phrase. That's because languages are built on needs and wants—not grammar and vocabulary.

Well before grammar school, we use language to get what we need or want. This is the reason children start talking. If screaming, crying, and making obnoxious sounds don't work, they will use language to get that cookie or ball or to help us see something they LOVE.

To start, look for phrases that grab your attention. For example, if you get in the car often and need everyone to buckle up, section "Car" under chapter C would be a great place to start.

If your siblings are constantly bothering you, "Don't" under chapter D is a great place to start. If you love to play with bubbles, "Bubbles" under chapter B would be a great place to start.

First, go through and mark your highest priorities, and learn those first. Then move on to secondary things.

Next, you just need to be a rebel. Don't pick Focus Phrases that aren't applicable to your family. Like, if you aren't changing diapers in your home or you don't tell your child, "No," skip those phrases. No need to email me with your parenting philosophy. I trust you to make the best choices for your family.

With that said, if you can add the phrase to your life—even if you don't say it in English, by all means, learn that phrase so that you can add it to your life and practice speaking Japanese.

Also, feel free to change phrases you wouldn't use by replacing them with other nouns you would use. For example, you might switch the word "baby bag" to "backpack." If you're using our boxes with this phrasebook, you'll find so many opportunities to mix and match a ton of phrases.

You can always go back to learn anything you skipped later. Maybe another baby will come into the picture. ☺

When you choose the Focus Phrase for your Phrase Practice Session, you can choose the phrase in front of your child, you can give your child two good options and allow them to choose the one that they're more excited about today, or you can let your child choose.

Have you or your child heart the phrase in the TalkBox.Mom Companion App for easy access to the audio and progress tracking.

Open your TalkBox.Mom Companion App included with your purchase or verified gifting of this book (see page 9 for instructions). Click on the book icon 📖 on the home screen. Then select Use Japanese at Home. After selecting the letter of the alphabet that coordinates with the section in which your phrase appears, slide the top section and click the bolded title that appears above or with your phrase.

Next, have you or your child click the heart ♥ next to the chosen phrases. Now your phrases will easily be accessed from the home screen under "Practicing." This will help save you time in the next steps!

For families with multiple children, you can alternate who hearts phrases or have your other children help in the following steps. If your child does not look at screens, they can listen to the audio without viewing your phone.

Step 2: Practice your Phrases

🕐 Time Needed: 2 minutes to 10 minutes

Note: The more phrases you've chosen, the longer this step will take.

For older children with required foreign language time of 30, 45, or 60 minutes a day, this step can expand to that time requirement, keeping in mind that Step 3 will give you additional time, especially as you're able to use more of the language.

The second step is to practice your chosen phrases. There are three main ways to practice your phrases, and they're listed here in order of importance: (1) practice with the native speaker audio, (2) practice in situations, and (3) practice with emotions.

❶ Practice the Phrase with the Native Speaker Audio

❝ That children should learn [Japanese] orally, by listening to and repeating [Japanese] words and phrases."- *Charlotte Mason*[6]

You might be tempted to skip this step if you, as the parent, can pronounce the phrases or if you're a native speaker, but don't skip it! It's important to have that extra input that's not just you. Get that extra input! There's a noticeable difference if you skip practicing with the native speaker audio.

To practice with the native speaker audio, navigate to your practicing section or the book in the TalkBox.Mom Companion App as described in the previous step. Be sure "autoplay" is turned off in the app because you want to practice one phrase at a time—not repeat all your phrases together.

> Have you or your child announce what the phrase is in English and tell everyone to repeat after the native speaker. For example, "We're going to hear how to say, 'Buckle up,' in Japanese. Have fun repeating after each word. If you can, say the full phrase after her at the end."

The native speaker will say the phrase word by word while pausing for your family to repeat. Then she will say the full phrase and pause for your family to repeat.

If the full phrase feels like too much at first, that's fine! Just say the phrase word by word. After a couple of days, you'll feel ready to say the entire phrase.

> After you finish repeating the phrase, have you or your child ask everyone what the phrase means. If some family members aren't sure, remind your family what it means, practice with the audio again, and ask again what the phrase means until everyone is on the same page.

When your family repeats with the audio, celebrate that everyone tried! Refrain from correcting anyone's pronunciation or being hard on yourself for how you sound.

Why? For family members over four years old, it can take a couple of weeks to a couple of months to hear the sounds in the new language, and when you can't hear the sounds, you can't fix the sounds. So if you tell someone they're saying it wrong, and they can't hear it to fix it, they'll just be annoyed with you.

But you can start hearing better as you're having fun as you listen and practice with the native speaker audio. The keyword here is fun! Stressed-out people have trouble hearing better. So be sure not to stress your kids or yourself out by focusing on sounding perfect.

Focus on having fun so you can continue to hear the sounds over time and improve as you continue to practice and use your phrases.

② Practice the Phrase in Situations

> Once your family repeats with the native speaker audio, practice that same phrase in a situation rather than moving on to the next phrase. You can absolutely play the audio again and again as you practice the phrase together.

To make this phrase real for your family and make your practice age-appropriate, decide together when you could add this phrase to your life. You can either set up that specific situation and practice using the phrase in that situation, use the phrase as you pretend you're in that situation, or say the phrase like you're in that situation. Yes, details immediately to follow.

For example, if the phrase is, "Follow the path," you could walk over to a path with your family and have one family member say the phrase and another family member follow the path. Then switch until everyone has had a turn to say the phrase!

Or you could pretend there is a path in your living room and have one family member say the phrase and another family member follow the path. Then switch until everyone has had a turn!

Or you could sit on the couch or ground outside (because it's just one of those days) and have a family member say the phrase like they see a path and want someone to follow it.

You can raise the stakes in any of these situations and say, "Say, 'Follow the path,' like you're on a secret mission in the jungle." Or, "Say, 'Follow the path,' like it leads to ice cream!" We call this game, "Say It Like." Let the creativity spill over here. Younger and older kids will have different ideas that match what's fun and interesting for their age level.

③ Practice the Phrase with Emotions

Here's where you can have even more fun! This is an extra important step if you've ever corrected your child's pronunciation, making them shut down or be less willing to try. And it's equally important if this has ever happened to you, and you have hesitations about speaking another language. Remember, it's more important to have fun than to sound perfect.

To practice with emotions, we have three outlets. The first is choosing raw emotions and having someone say a phrase with that emotion.

For example, "Say the phrase, 'Follow the path,' like you're really happy!"

You can choose any emotion or state, like excited, sleepy, scared, nervous, creepy, or hangry.

The second way to practice emotions is by saying the phrase like you're someone else. Choose a person your child knows. This could be a friend, superhero, or character. For example, "Say the phrase, 'Follow the path,' like Grandma."

The third way to practice a phrase with emotions is with music! Different styles of music can make you feel different ways. You could sing your phrase like an opera singer or rap artist. Whatever musical style you or your child likes or wants to try. And you don't have to be on tune to make this jam session effective.

> After you practice your phrase, go back to Part 1 and listen to your next phrase repeating these two steps.

Q: What should I do if my child is an infant or toddler?

A: Practice and use your phrases around your infant or toddler! He or she doesn't need to repeat with the audio or practice saying the phrases yet to learn. This is a great age for them to take in what you're doing and learn from you.

Step 3: Use the Phrases

At this point, "lesson time" is over, and real life begins!

> It only be a little lesson, ten minutes long, and the slight break and the effort of attention will give the greater zest to the pleasure and leisure to follow."
> - *Charlotte Mason*[7]

> Now it's time to encourage everyone to try to add your phrases to your day as many times as you can before your next Phrase Practice Session!

Celebrate any attempt at using phrases. Even if only a word or two come out!

If you forget to use a phrase and remember it moments later, use it right then! Start building that habit.

And please! Don't deprive yourself of looking at the phrase or listening to the audio again to help you say that phrase. You might feel like you're cheating or like you need to force yourself to remember. Nope. Make it very easy for yourself until it feels like second nature. If it doesn't feel like second nature, you need to look and listen again to continue to build that neural pathway.

Now, if someone in your family uses one of your phrases and another family member forgets what the phrase means, tell them what it means! You want to make it easy for your children to know what's going on. They just put in all the work to learn their first language, which now feels super easy to them. If the second language feels difficult, there can be more resistance.

So say the phrase in English if someone is confused and then again in the language that you're learning. We call this the "Ice Cream Sandwich" because you first say the phrase in the other language, then in English to clarify, and then in the other language again.

As you use your phrases as a family, our goal is fun—not perfection. The fastest way to improve is to elevate the journey— not the finish line.

If you have a family member who already speaks Japanese and is constantly correcting or just sometimes corrects you... or you want to make sure you are on the same page, ask him or her to read the love letter on the next page.

Dear smart and clever Japanese speaker of the beautiful person who came over to you, asking you to read this,

    I know it's really hard, so please try your best to avoid nitpicking at how your family pronounces and says things in Japanese, and also please refrain from correcting every little thing. I know you want to help, and, as you might know, constant correction will not actually help your loved ones to learn. It will silently break their hearts, make them angry with you, and make them want to quit.

Instead, continue to talk to your family in Japanese and answer their questions. It will help them so much. Over time, in their time, they will learn from your example as well as from their Practice Sessions with this phrasebook. Plus, you will score major points for being nice, positive, and patient. Yes, of course, you're welcome.

Your Daily Schedule

> "The daily [Japanese] lesson is one that should not be omitted." - *Charlotte Mason*[8]

As your next Practice Session starts in two hours or the next day—depending on the speed you want to progress—check off the phrase(s) from your previous Practice Session to indicate that you practiced the phrase(s).

Record your previous Focus Phrases from the phrasebook in sets of 10 phrases max. Before each Practice Session, quickly review a set of previous Focus Phrases by either practicing the phrase with an emotion or in a situation as you play the audio. It should take 10 - 15 seconds to review each phrase.

Then complete your next Practice Session, and work together as a family to use the phrase(s) as much as you can.

Remember, to quickly hear a Focus Phrase again and again, click "Practicing" on the home screen of the app where your hearted phrase is saved.

> 66

Previously, we were using Japanese, reading Japanese picture books, singing Japanese nursery songs, and enrolled our oldest in Japanese preschool, but after 1 WEEK of TalkBox.Mom, my 5 and 3 year old are speaking more Japanese than I have heard from them since they started talking.

- Tina Burel -

Our family is having such fun speaking to each other and challenging each other. I didn't expect the family-building, family-strengthening benefits that would come from this.

- Kathryn Winterscheidt -

We've only been learning Japanese for about 2 weeks, and my son is consistently asking how to say things in Japanese. He just asked me for cereal in Japanese and wanted to ask for more. We learned it, and he got more cereal!

- Samantha Sanders -

My husband is fluent in Japanese. Today, after hearing my kids and I discuss food in Japanese, he commented, "You know, at first I was skeptical. But this program is really working." We are actually communicating with each other. They've developed a much stronger interest in Japanese than ever before. My husband is thoroughly converted, and I'm a HUGE fan.

- Melanie Schaab -

You're Invited!

The TalkBox.Mom boxes, our signature program, are excellent to use along with your phrasebook because you'll make more progress using them together—without adding any extra strain to your day.

Each box has a different fluency approach than the phrasebook. For example, the fluency approach of the first box, the Snacks & Kitchen Box, is consistency and exponential progress.

To create consistency, we not only link speaking Japanese to a specific activity you do daily, but we also link it to a specific area in your home. To help you make exponential progress, the patterns that we chose for your family lay a strong foundation of the language and open you up to being able to say more than

USE JAPANESE AT HOME

31

just the phrases you're focusing on.

And like I said, you'll spend the same amount of time practicing phrases. Your Practice Sessions will still have 1-5 Focus Phrases. However, you'll pick the bulk of your phrases from your boxes.

In the phrasebook, you skip topic to topic rather quickly. However, each box focuses on a specific topic and each Challenge narrows that focus to create a full sequence. With these sequences, you learn phrases faster and go deeper.

With that said, the phrasebook has such varied phrases that this keeps foreign language exciting and allows you to add more varied phrases to your life. This is the perfect complement to the patterns you find in the boxes. For this reason, you'll find that you'll use the phrasebook throughout all nine of the boxes.

As you use the phrasebook with the boxes, you'll start hearing your family use Japanese throughout your entire day.

How do the boxes work?

Each box has three Challenges with a different language guide for each Challenge. The language guide might be a sequence of phrases, a poster mixing and matching full phrases, label cards with full phrases to use common items in your home, or an activity to do with your family.

You'll spend one week to one month per Challenge. During that time, your goal is to complete at least 10 Phrase Practice Sessions. If you're competitive and complete more Practice Sessions during that time, then awesome!

After at least 10 Phrase Practice Sessions, you move on to your next Challenge in the box. You don't learn every phrase in your Challenge. Rather, you start with high-priority phrases and work your way down. And when you come back to a Challenge later, because you've been using your phrases, you learn the rest of the phrases even faster. Yes, faster than if you tried to learn every single phrase before moving on.

After you complete at least 10 Phrase Practice Sessions for each Challenge, move on to your next box!

Boxes can be delivered once a month, every two months, or every three months. It's also possible to pick your own delivery dates or pause based on your needs—like if you're going to Japan to use your Japanese, you can have a couple of boxes delivered together to take with you and choose a date further out for your next box.

With each box, you facilitate a high-level immersion experience that would cost at least $750 <u>each time</u> you work through a box <u>per person</u>. We put that experience into a $90 box for your family. And if you love to save money, you can pre-purchase all your boxes and save.

So if you'd like to go even deeper in Japanese and have more fun with us, I'd love to invite you to purchase your first box or all nine.

Go to **www.talkbox.mom/japanese** and checkout with the same email address you purchased the book so that all your programs are together!

After that, you'll be invited to an exclusive bonus for our signature program: our Accountability Community. Here you'll be able to share your progress as you work through your Challenges, get ideas for your Practice Sessions in the boxes, and connect with other families who are learning to use Japanese together!

I can't wait to see you there!

What The Banner?

> WHAT ARE THESE LITTLE BANNERS THROUGHOUT THE BOOK?

These banners let you know where we go deeper into these topics in the TalkBox.Mom signature program.

The phrasebook can be used on its own or—for an elevated experience—it can be used with the boxes.

The second is my favorite because you're able to use the language more consistently and make exponential progress due to the various fluency approaches used in the boxes. Plus, with the phrasebook, you're able to add phrases from different topics, mixing and matching phrases from the phrasebook with the grammar patterns you've mastered with phrases in the boxes.

I've sprinkled these banners throughout the book so you can see where we go deeper in the signature program and decide if you're ready to take the plunge of a lifetime.

Go to **www.talkbox.mom/japanese** to join us!

Add Japanese *phrases* to your *daily life.*

More details on page 17.

→

🚫 **Don't read from A - Z.** Learn first what you need to say, want to say, and say all the time.

🔊 **Native speaker audio for every phrase!** See Page 9.

▣ **You'll find notes next to some phrases.** Find out how to use (*for a male* / *female*) and more.

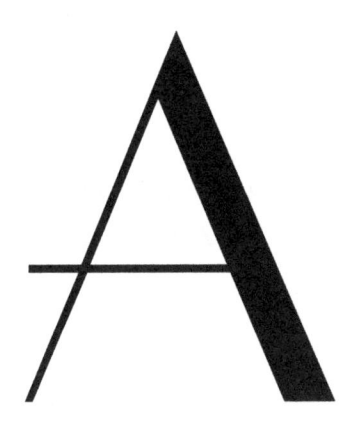

A

learn it!

♥ ☑ *Got it!*

♡ ☐ **Again!** **もう一回!**
Mou ikkai!

♡ ☐ Try again. もう一回やってみよう。
Mou ikkai yattemiyou.

♡ ☐ Do you want to play again? また遊びたい？
Mata asobitai?

♡ ☐ Let's play again. また遊ぼうね。
Mata asoboune.

♡ ☐ I want to watch the video again. その動画もう一回観たい。
Sono douga mou ikkai mitai.

♡ ☐ I need to change your diaper again. またオムツ替えなきゃね。
Mata omutsu kaenakyane.

USE JAPANESE AT HOME

A

♥ ☑
♡ ☐ Please wash your hands again. もう一回手を洗って。
Mou ikkai tewo aratte.

♡ ☐ **All done!** ぜんぶやった！
Zenbu yatta!

♡ ☐ Finished! 終わったよ！
Owattayo!

♡ ☐ I'm all done. 全部やったよ。
Zenbu yattayo.

♡ ☐ Are you all done eating? 食べ終わった？
Tabe owatta?

♡ ☐ Are you all done taking a bath? もうお風呂終わりかな？
Mou ofuro owari kana?

♡ ☐ I can tell that you are all done. *(after eating)* もうおしまいでいいね。
Mou oshimaide iine.

♡ ☐ *(assignment or task)* 全部やったね。
Zenbu yattane.

GET LANGUAGE GUIDES FOR SNACKS, DRINKS, MEALS, AND DINING IN THE TALKBOX.MOM SUBSCRIPTION

A

All gone! もうないよ!
Mou naiyo!

The water is all gone. お水はもうないよ。
Omizuwa mou naiyo.

There is no more water left. もうお水は残ってないよ。
Mou omizuwa nokotte naiyo.

The (potato) chips are all gone. (ポテト)チップスはもうないよ。
(Poteto) chippusuwa mou naiyo.

The sweets are all gone. お菓子はもうないよ。
Okashiwa mou naiyo.

There are no more (potato) chips left. もう(ポテト)チップスは残ってないよ。
Mou (poteto) chippusuwa nokotte naiyo.

There are no more sweets left. お菓子はもう残ってないよ。
Okashiwa mou nokotte naiyo

USE JAPANESE AT HOME

B

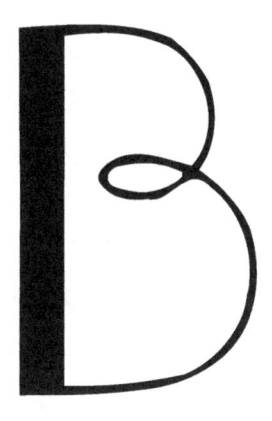

learn it!

♥ ☑ *Got it!*

	the baby bag *(mama bag)*	マザーズバッグ **mazaazu baggu**
♡ ☐	I need to pack the baby bag.	マザーズバッグの準備しなきゃ。 Mazaazu bagguno junbi shinakya.
♡ ☐	Did you pull everything out of the baby bag?	マザーズバッグから、持ち物全部出した？ Mazaazu baggukara mochimono zenbu dashita?
♡ ☐	Where is the baby bag?	マザースバッグ、どこにある？ Mazzazu baggu dokoni aru?
♡ ☐	I can't find the baby bag.	マザーズバッグが見つからない。 Mazaazu bagguga mitsukaranai.

USE JAPANESE AT HOME

B

♥☑		
♡☐	Would you please help me find the baby bag?	マザーズバッグ探すの手伝ってくれる？ Mazaazu baggu sagasuno tetsudatte kureru?
♡☐	Help me find the baby bag, please.	マザーズバッグ探すの手伝って。 Mazaazu baggu sagasuno tetsudatte.
♡☐	It's in the baby bag.	マザーズバッグに入ってるよ。 Mazaazu bagguni haitteruyo.
♡☐	Are the wipes in the baby bag?	おしりふきは、マザーズバッグに入ってる？ Oshirifukuwa mazaazu baggu ni haitteru?
♡☐	I think so.	そうだと思うよ。 Sou dato omouyo.

	the babysitter	**子守り** **komori**
♡☐	(*Name*) is babysitting tonight.	今晩は(*name*)さんが、お世話しに来てくれるよ。 Konbanwa (*name*)sanga osewashini kite kureruyo.
♡☐	The babysitter is here.	(*Name*)が来たよ。 (*Name*)ga kitayo.

42 TALKBOX.MOM

B

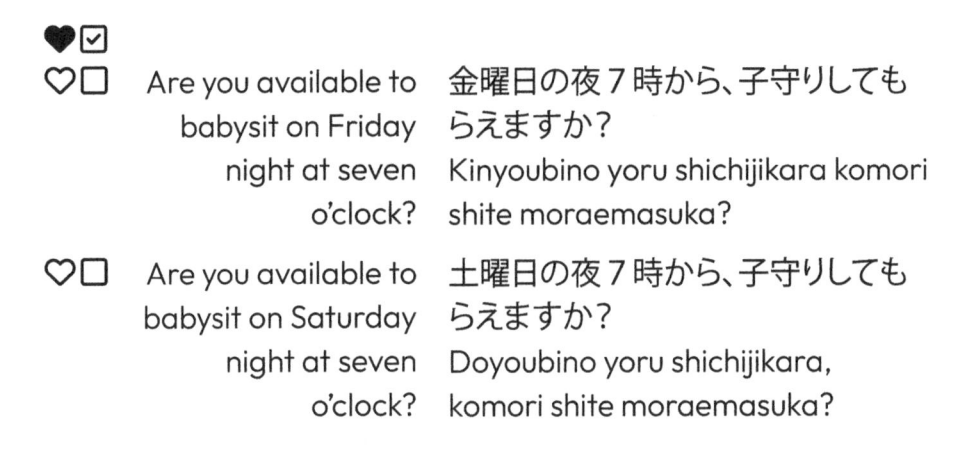

Are you available to babysit on Friday night at seven o'clock?
金曜日の夜7時から、子守りしてもらえますか？
Kinyoubino yoru shichijikara komori shite moraemasuka?

Are you available to babysit on Saturday night at seven o'clock?
土曜日の夜7時から、子守りしてもらえますか？
Doyoubino yoru shichijikara, komori shite moraemasuka?

> GET LABEL CARDS FOR ROOMS AND AREAS IN YOUR HOME IN THE TALKBOX.MOM SUBSCRIPTION

the backyard お庭
oniwa

Do you want to play in the backyard?
お庭で遊びたい？
Oniwade asobitai?

Let's play in the backyard.
お庭で遊ぼうよ。
Oniwade asobouyo.

The kids are in the backyard.
子供達は、お庭にいるよ。
Kodomotachiwa oniwani iruyo.

I left my (toy) car in the backyard.
車、お庭においてきちゃった。
Kuruma oniwani oitekichatta.

I left my doll in the backyard.
お人形、お庭においてきちゃった。
Oningyo oniwani oitekichatta.

USE JAPANESE AT HOME

B

♥ ☑
♡ ☐ Did you leave your bike in the backyard? 自転車、お庭においてきちゃったの？
Jitensha oniwani oitekichattano?

♡ ☐ Go put it away. *(the bike)* 片付けてきなさい。
Katazukete kinasai.

bad いけないこと
ikenaikoto

♡ ☐ I did something bad. いけないことしちゃったんだ。
Ikenaikoto shichattanda.

♡ ☐ That was bad. それは、ダメだね。
Sorewa damedane.

the ball ボール
booru

♡ ☐ Let's play with the ball. ボールで遊ぼう。
Boorude asobou.

♡ ☐ Do you want to play with the ball? ボールで遊びたい？
Boorude asobitai?

♡ ☐ Take the ball. ボール取って。
Booru totte.

♡ ☐ Give me the ball. ボールをちょうだい。
Booru watashite.

B

♥☑			
♡☐	Hand me the ball.	ボール渡して。 Booru watashite.	
♡☐	Roll the ball.	ボール転がして。 Booru korogashite.	
♡☐	I got it.	取ったよ。 Tottayo.	
♡☐	You got it.	取ったね。 Tottane.	
♡☐	Put the ball down.	ボールを置いて。 Booru hirotte.	
♡☐	Pick up the ball.	ボール拾って。 Booru hirotte.	
♡☐	Throw the ball.	ボール投げて。 Booru nagete.	
♡☐	Catch the ball.	ボール取って。 Booru totte.	
♡☐	You caught the ball!	ボール取ったね! Booru tottane!	
♡☐	I missed it.	ああ、おしい。 Aa oshii.	
♡☐	I caught the ball!	ボール取ったよ! Booru tottayo!	
♡☐	Good catch!	上手に取れたね! Joozuni toretane!	
♡☐	Nice throw!	上手に投げたね! Joozuni nagetane!	

USE JAPANESE AT HOME

B

♥ ☑

♡ ☐ Get the ball. ボール取って。
Booru totte.

♡ ☐ Kick the ball. ボール蹴って。
Booru kette.

♡ ☐ The ball went under the couch. ボールがソファーの下に入っちゃった。
Booruga sofaano shitani haicchatta.

♡ ☐ Don't throw the ball in the house. 家の中でボール投げないで。
Ieno nakade booru nagenaide.

♡ ☐ Play with your ball outside. ボール遊びは、外でしてね。
Booruasobiwa sotode shitene.

the balloon 風船
fuusen

♡ ☐ Look at the balloons! 風船見て！
Fuusen mite!

♡ ☐ I'm blowing up balloons. 風船、膨らましてるの。
Fuusen fukuramashiteruno.

♡ ☐ Help me blow up the balloons. 風船、膨らますの手伝って。
Fuusen fukuramasuno tetsudatte.

♡ ☐ Don't put the balloon in your mouth. 風船を口の中に入れちゃダメ。
Fuusenwo kuchino nakani irecha dame.

B

♥ ☑
♡ ☐ I'm sorry. You cannot have a balloon. — ごめんね。風船はもらえないよ。
Gomenne. Fuusenwa moraenaiyo.

the Band-Aid® バンそうこう
bansoko

♡ ☐ Do you want a Band-Aid®? — ばんそうこう、欲しい？
Bansoko hoshii?

♡ ☐ I need a Band-Aid®! — ばんそうこう、要る！
Bansoko iru!

♡ ☐ Leave your Band-Aid® on. — ばんそうこう、剥がさないでね。
Bansoko hagasanaidene.

the basket バスケット
basuketto

♡ ☐ Put your toys in the basket. — バスケットにおもちゃしまって。
Basukettoni omocha shimatte.

♡ ☐ The basket is empty. — バスケットは空っぽだよ。
Basukettowa karappodayo.

♡ ☐ Don't stand on the basket. — バスケットに乗っちゃダメ。
Basukettoni noccha dame.

♡ ☐ You're breaking it. — 壊れちゃうでしょ。
Kowarechaudesho.

USE JAPANESE AT HOME

B

the bath お風呂
ofuro

It's bath time. お風呂の時間だよ。
Ofurono jikandayo.

Did you take a bath already? もうお風呂入ったの？
Mou ofuro haittano?

You need to take a bath. お風呂入らなきゃ。
Ofuro hairanakya.

It's your turn to give the kids a bath. 子供たちをお風呂に入れる番でしょ。
Kodomotachiwo ofuroni ireru ban desho.

It's your turn to give him/her a bath. (Name)をお風呂に入れる番でしょ。
(Name)wo ofuroni ireru ban desho.

> BATHING WALL CHART, HYGIENE GUIDES & BATHROOM LABEL CARDS IN THE TALKBOX.MOM SUBSCRIPTION

the batteries 電池
denchi

The toy needs batteries. このおもちゃは、電池が必要なんだね。
Kono omochawa denchiga hitsuyou nandane.

B

♥☑		The batteries are dead.	電池が切れちゃってるね。 Denchiga kirechatterune.
♡☐		I need to put new batteries in your toy.	おもちゃに新しい電池入れなきゃ。 Omochani atarashii denchi irenakya.
♡☐		I put new batteries in your toy.	おもちゃに新しい電池入れたよ。 Omochani atarashii denchi iretayo.
♡☐		We need to buy some batteries.	電池買わなきゃ。 Denchi kawanakya.
♡☐		Do not put the battery in your mouth.	電池を口に入れちゃダメ。 Denchiwo kuchini irecha dame.
♡☐		You may not play with batteries.	電池で遊んではいけません。 Denchide asondewa ikemasen.

the bed ベッド
beddo
(written beddo, pronounced betto)

the futon* 布団
futon

♡☐	You need to make your bed.	ベッドきれいにしてね。 Beddo kireini shitene.

*Japanese children usually sleep on a futon, which is a little mattress that they roll out on the floor and put away in the morning.

USE JAPANESE AT HOME

B

- [x] Don't jump on the bed. — ベッドの上で飛び跳ねちゃダメ。 Beddono uede tobihanecha dame.
- [ ] Don't eat food in your bed. — ベッドの上で食べちゃダメ。 Beddono uede tabecha dame.
- [ ] Did you wet the bed? — おねしょしちゃった？ Onesho shichatta?

- [ ] **Bed time!** — **寝る時間！ Neru jikan!**
- [ ] It's time for bed. — 寝る時間だよ。 Neru jikan dayo.
- [ ] Get in your bed. — ベッドに入って。 Beddoni haitte.
- [ ] Please tell me/us a story before bed. — 寝る前にお話しして。 Nerumaeni ohanashishite.
- [ ] Good night! — おやすみなさい！ Oyasuminasai!
- [ ] I love you.* — 大好きだよ。 Daisukidayo.
- [ ] Stay in your bed. / futon. — ちゃんとベッド / お布団 に入ってて。 Chanto beddo / ofuton ni haittete.

*Japanese families do not commonly say, "I love you," to their children. They just say, "Good night," at bedtime.

B

♥☑

♡☐	Don't get out of your bed. / futon.	ベッド/お布団 から出ちゃダメ。 Beddo / Ofuton kara dechadame.
♡☐	Stop playing, and lie down please.	遊ぶのやめて、ちゃんと横になってて。 Asobuno yamete chanto yokoninattete.
♡☐	Go back in your bed. / futon.	ベッド/お布団 に戻って。 Beddo / ofuton ni modotte.
♡☐	Go back to your room(s).	部屋に戻って。 Heyani modotte.
♡☐	You can't fall asleep if you are not lying down.	ちゃんと横になってないと、眠れないよ。 Chanto yokoni nattenaito nemurenaiyo.
♡☐	Please go to sleep.	寝てください。 Nete kudasai.
♡☐	The kids are finally asleep.	子供達、やっと寝た。 Kodomotachi yatto neta.
♡☐	The baby is finally asleep.	赤ちゃん、やっと寝てくれた。 Akachan yatto netekureta.

B

the bib スタイ / エプロン
(*in a store / at home*) **sutai / epuron**

Here's your bib. エプロン、どうぞ。
Epuron douzo.

Do you want your bib off? エプロン取りたいの？
Epuron toritaino?

You need to keep your bib on. エプロン、つけてなきゃダメ。
Epuron tsuketenakya dame.

the Bible 聖書
seisho

It's time to read the Bible. 聖書を読む時間だよ。
Seishowo yomu jikan dayo.

Come sit down. We're reading the Bible together. こっちに来て座って。一緒に聖書を読もうね。
Kocchini kite suwatte. Isshoni seishowo yomoune.

big 大きい
ookii

Do you want the big car or the little car? 大きい車と小さい車、どっちが欲しい？
Ookii kuruma to chiisai kuruma docchiga hoshii?

B

- ♥ ☑
- ♡ ☐ I'm a big boy. ぼくはおにいちゃん。
  Bokuwa oniichan.
- ♡ ☐ I'm a big girl. 私はおねえちゃん。
  Watashiwa oneechan.

the bike 自転車
jitensha

- ♡ ☐ Do you want to ride your bike? 自転車乗りたい？
  Jitensha noritai?
- ♡ ☐ I want to ride my bike. 自転車乗りたい。
  Jitensha noritai.
- ♡ ☐ Let's ride our bikes. 自転車に乗ろうか。
  Jitenshani norouka.
- ♡ ☐ Where did you leave your bike? 自転車どこに置いたの？
  Jitensha dokoni oitano?
- ♡ ☐ Where is your bike? 自転車どこ？
  Jitensha doko?
- ♡ ☐ Outside. 外。
  Soto.
- ♡ ☐ In the yard. お庭。
  Oniwa.
- ♡ ☐ In the garage. ガレージ。
  Gareeji.

B

♥ ☑
♡ ☐ Please put your bike away.
自転車、片付けて。
Jitensha katazukete.

the binky おしゃぶり
oshaburi

♡ ☐ Where is the binky?
おしゃぶり、どこ？
Oshaburi doko?

♡ ☐ I can't find the binky.
おしゃぶりが見つからない。
Oshaburiga mitsukaranai.

♡ ☐ It's missing.
なくなっちゃった。
Nakunacchatta.

♡ ☐ Here's your binky.
おしゃぶり、あったよ。
Oshaburi attayo.

to bite 噛む
kamu

♡ ☐ Take a bite of your sandwich.
サンドイッチ、一口食べて。
Sandoicchi hitokuchi tabete.

♡ ☐ Three more bites.
あと3口食べて。
Ato mikuchi tabete.

♡ ☐ Don't bite me. *(for a mother)*
ママのこと噛まないで。
Mamanokoto kamanaide.

B

♥ ☑			
♡ ☐	Don't bite me. (*for a father*)	パパのこと噛まないで。	Papanokoto kamanaide.
♡ ☐	Don't bite me. (*for a female*)	私のこと噛まないで。	Watashinokoto kamanaide.
♡ ☐	(*for a male*)	ぼくのこと噛まないで。	Bokunokoto kamanaide.
♡ ☐	Don't bite your (*older*) sister.	おねえちゃん噛んじゃダメ。	Oneechan kanja dame.
♡ ☐	Don't bite your (*younger*) sister.	妹噛んじゃダメ。	Imouto kanja dame.
♡ ☐	Don't bite your (*older*) brother.	お兄ちゃん噛んじゃダメ。	Oniichan kanja dame.
♡ ☐	Don't bite your (*younger*) brother.	弟噛んじゃダメ。	Otouto kanja dame.
♡ ☐	Don't bite her/him.	(*Name*) 噛んじゃダメ。	(*Name*) kanja dame.
♡ ☐	No biting.	噛まないよ。	Kamanai yo.
♡ ☐	She/He bit me!	(*Name*)が噛んだ!	(*Name*)ga kanda!

USE JAPANESE AT HOME

B

the blanket 毛布 / お布団
(blanket / blanky) **moufu / ofuton**

	Here is your blanket.	毛布、どうぞ。 Moufu douzo.
	Where did you put your blanket?	毛布、どこにやっちゃったの？ Moufu dokoni yacchattano?
	I can't sleep without my blanket. (for a female)	私の毛布がないと眠れない。 Watashino moufuga naito nemurenai.
	(for a male)	ぼくの毛布がないと眠れない。 Bokuno moufuga naito nemurenai.
	I found your blanket.	毛布が見つかった。 Moufuga mitsukatta.
	Don't drag your blanket on the ground.	毛布引きずらないで。 Moufu hikizuranaide.
	Bless you!*	*In Japan, people do not say "Bless you!" after someone sneezes. Instead, they respectfully ignore that the person sneezed.

B

the blocks ブロック
burokku

Let's play with your blocks. ブロックで遊ぼう。
Burokkude asobou.

Let's make a giant tower. おっきなタワーを作ろう。
Okkina tawaawo tsukurou.

Please hand me a block. ブロック、取って。
Burokku totte.

Wow! You made a huge tower. すごい！おっきなタワー作ったね。
Sugoi! Okkina tawaa tsukuttane.

Don't knock over my tower. *(for a female)* 私のタワー壊さないで。
Watashino tawaa kowasanaide.

(for a male) ぼくのタワー壊さないで。
Bokuno tawaa kowasanaide.

He/She knocked over my tower. *(for a female)* (Name)が私のタワー壊した。
(Name)ga watashino tawaa kowashita.

(for a male) (Name)がぼくのタワー壊した。
(Name)ga bokuno tawaa kowashita.

Let's knock over the tower. タワー、壊しちゃおう。
Tawaa kowashichaou.

Please put your blocks away. ブロック、片付けて。
Burokku katazukete.

B

the blood 血
chi

I'm bleeding. 血が出てる。
Chiga deteru.

He/She is bleeding a lot. (Name) すごく血が出てるよ。
(Name) sugoku chiga deteruyo.

He/She bled a little bit. (Name) ちょっとだけ血が出たみたい。
(Name) chottodake chiga detamitai.

Don't touch the blood. 血触っちゃダメ。
Chi sawaccha dame.

My nose is bleeding. 鼻血が出てる。
Hanajiga deteru.

Blow! 吹く!
Fuku!

Blow on your food. フーフーして食べて。
Fuu fuu shite tabete.

It's hot. 熱いよ。
Atsuiyo.

Blow out your candles! ろうそくフーって消して!
Rousoku fuutte keshite!

Don't blow out your (older) brother's candles. お兄ちゃんのろうそく、消しちゃダメ。
Oniichanno rousoku keshicha dame.

B

- Don't blow out your (*younger*) brother's candles. 弟のろうそく、消しちゃダメ。
Otoutono rousoku keshicha dame.

- Don't blow out your (*older*) sister's candles. お姉ちゃんのろうそく、消しちゃダメ。
Oneechanno rousoku keshicha dame.

- Don't blow out your (*younger*) sister's candles. 妹のろうそく、消しちゃダメ。
Imoutono rousoku keshicha dame.

- Blow your nose with a tissue. ティッシュで鼻かんで。
Tisshude hana kande.

the boat お船
ofune

- Here is your boat. お船、どうぞ。
Ofune douzo.

- You can take your boat in the bathtub. お船、お風呂に持っていってもいいよ。
Ofune ofuroni motteittemo iiyo.

B

♥ ☑ **the boogers** 鼻くそ
hanakuso

♡ ☐ You have a booger. 鼻くそがついてるよ。
Hanakusoga tsuiteruyo.

♡ ☐ Don't pick your nose. 鼻ほじっちゃダメ。
Hana hojiccha dame.

♡ ☐ Blow your nose. 鼻かんで。
Hana kande.

♡ ☐ Blow your nose with a tissue. ティッシュで鼻かんで。
Tisshude hana kande.

♡ ☐ Don't wipe your boogers on your shirt. シャツでお鼻拭いちゃダメ。
Shatsude ohana fuicha dame.

♡ ☐ Don't flick your boogers. 鼻くそ飛ばさないで。
Hanakuso tobasanaide.

♡ ☐ Don't eat your boogers. 鼻くそ、食べちゃダメ。
Hanakuso tabecha dame.

the book 本
hon

(to babies and toddlers) ご本
gohon

♡ ☐ Let's read together? 一緒に本読もうか？
Isshoni hon yomouka?

B

♥ ☑			
♡ ☐	(to babies and toddlers)	一緒にご本読もうか?	Isshoni gohon yomouka?
♡ ☐	Let's read together.	一緒に本読もうね。	Isshoni hon yomoune.
♡ ☐	(to babies and toddlers)	一緒にご本読もうね。	Isshoni gohon yomoune.
♡ ☐	Which book do you want to read?	どの本読みたい?	Dono hon yomitai?
♡ ☐	(to babies and toddlers)	どのご本読みたい?	Dono gohon yomitai?
♡ ☐	Did you like the book? (Did you like the story?)	この話好きだった?	Kono hanashi sukidatta?
♡ ☐	(to babies and toddlers)	このお話好きだった?	Kono ohanashi sukidatta?
♡ ☐	I liked the book. (I liked the story.)	この話好き。	Kono hanashi suki.
♡ ☐	(for babies and toddlers)	このお話好き。	Kono ohanashi suki.

USE JAPANESE AT HOME

B

❤️ ☑️

	the bottle	ボトル
		botoru
	the baby bottle *(the milk)*	ミルク
		miruku

♡ ☐ I need to give the baby a bottle. 赤ちゃんにミルクあげないと。
Akachanni miruku agenaito.

♡ ☐ Would you please give the baby a bottle? 赤ちゃんにミルクあげてくれる？
Akachanni miruku agetekureru?

♡ ☐ It's time for your bottle. ミルクの時間だよ。
Mirukuno jikan dayo.

♡ ☐ Don't forget your water bottle. お水のボトル忘れないで。
Omizuno botoru wasurenaide.

GET A LANGUAGE GUIDE FOR BREASTFEEDING & BOTTLES IN THE TALKBOX.MOM SUBSCRIPTION

---

	the box	箱
		hako
	the toy box	おもちゃ箱
		omochabako
	the large box	大きい箱
		ookii hako

B

the small box　小さい箱
chiisai hako

- ♡ ☐ Please put your toys in the box.　おもちゃ、箱に入れてね。
  Omocha hakoni iretene.

- ♡ ☐ Are you hiding in the box?　箱の中に隠れてるの？
  Hakono nakani kakureteruno?

- ♡ ☐ Take the lid off the box.　箱のフタを開けて。
  Hakono futawo akete.

- ♡ ☐ Put the lid on the box.　箱のフタを閉めて。
  Hakono futawo shimete.

- ♡ ☐ Open the box.　箱、開けて。
  Hako akete.

- ♡ ☐ Close the box.　箱、閉めて。
  Hako shimete.

- ♡ ☐ Let me open the box.　箱、開けてあげる。
  Hako aketeageru.

- ♡ ☐ Let me close the box.　箱、閉めてあげる。
  Hako shimeteageru.

- ♡ ☐ Your ball is in the box.　ボールは、箱の中にあるよ。
  Booruwa hakono nakani aruyo.

B

to break 壊す
(stop functioning) **kowasu**
(into pieces) 割る
waru

	What did I just hear break?	今のは何が壊れた音？ Imanowa naniga kowareta oto?
	Who broke the vase?	誰が花瓶割ったの？ Darega kabin wattano?
	Who broke the window?	誰が窓割ったの？ Darega mado wattano?
	Who broke the toy?	誰がおもちゃ壊したの？ Darega omocha kowashitano?
	Who broke the plate?	誰がお皿割ったの？ Darega osara wattano?
	I broke the plate. *(for a female)*	私がお皿割っちゃったの。 Watashiga osara wacchattano.
	(for a male)	ぼくがお皿割っちゃったの。 Bokuga osara wacchattano.
	The chair broke.	椅子が壊れちゃった。 Isuga kowarechatta.
	The toy is broken.	そのおもちゃ、壊れてる。 Sono omocha kowareteru.

B

to take a break 休憩
kyuukei

Let's take a break. ちょっと休憩しよう。
Chotto kyuukei shiyou.

You need to take a little break. ちょっと休憩しなきゃダメ。
Chotto kyuukei shinakya dame.

to breastfeed おっぱいをあげる
oppaiwo ageru

I need to nurse the baby. 赤ちゃんにおっぱいあげなきゃ。
Akachanni oppai agenakya.

I need to nurse the baby in fifteen minutes. 十五分したら、赤ちゃんにおっぱいあげなきゃ。
Juugofun shitara akachanni oppai agenakya.

I need to nurse the baby in one hour. 一時間したら、赤ちゃんにおっぱいあげなきゃ。
Ichijikan shitara akachanni oppai agenakya.

I need to nurse the baby in two hours 二時間したら、赤ちゃんにおっぱいあげなきゃ。
Nijikan shitara akachanni oppai agenakya.

> GET A LANGUAGE GUIDE FOR BREASTFEEDING & BOTTLES IN THE TALKBOX.MOM SUBSCRIPTION

USE JAPANESE AT HOME

B

the broom ほうき
houki

I need to sweep the floor.	床を掃かなきゃ。 Yukawo hakanakya.
Please hand me the broom.	ほうきちょうだい。 Houki choudai.
Where is the dustpan?	ちりとりはどこ？ Chiritoriwa doko?
Sweep the trash into the dustpan.	ゴミを掃いてちりとりに入れて。 Gomiwo haite chiritorini irete.
Put the trash into the trash can.	ゴミをゴミ箱に入れて。 Gomiwo gomibakoni irete.
I already swept the floor.	もう床、掃いたよ。 Mou yuka haitayo.
Don't make a mess.	散らかさないで。 Chirakasanaide.
I just swept the floor!	ちょうど今、床を掃いたところ！ Choudo ima, yukawo haita tokoro!

to brush hair 髪をとかす
kamiwo tokasu

Let's brush your hair.	髪の毛とかそうね。 Kaminoke tokasoune.

B

♥ ☑
♡ ☐   Please brush your hair.   髪の毛とかしてね。
Kaminoke tokashitene.

> STEP BY STEP LANGUAGE GUIDE FOR BRUSHING TEETH WITH CHILDREN IN THE TALKBOX.MOM SUBSCRIPTION

to brush teeth   歯を磨く
hawo migaku

♡ ☐   Let's brush your teeth.   歯磨きしよう。
Hamigaki shiyou.

♡ ☐   Please brush your teeth.   歯磨きしてね。
Hamigaki shitene.

the bubbles   シャボン玉
shabondama

♡ ☐   Let's play with bubbles!   シャボン玉で遊ぼう!
Shabondamade asobou!

♡ ☐   Pop the bubbles!   シャボン玉膨らまそう!
Shabondama fukuramasou!

♡ ☐   Blow some more bubbles.   もっとシャボン玉飛ばそう。
Motto shabondama tobasou.

♡ ☐   Do you want me to blow some bubbles?   シャボン玉飛ばしてほしい?
Shabondama tobashite hoshii?

USE JAPANESE AT HOME

B

♥☑			
♡☐	Don't blow so hard.	そんなに強く吹かないで。 Sonnani tsuyoku fukanaide.	
♡☐	Blow soft, and it will work.	優しくフーってすれば、できるよ。 Yasashiku fuutte sureba dekiruyo.	
♡☐	Dip the wand in again.	シャボン玉液もう一回つけて。 Shabondamaeki mouikkai tsukete.	
♡☐	Put the wand in the bubbles.	棒にシャボン玉液つけて。 Bouni shabondamaeki tsukete.	
♡☐	Close the lid.	ふた、閉めて。 Futa shimete.	

the bucket バケツ
baketsu

♡☐	Put the rocks in the bucket.	石をバケツの中に入れて。 Ishiwo baketsuno nakani irete.
♡☐	Let's fill the bucket up with water.	バケツにお水いっぱい入れよう。 Baketsuni omizu ippai ireyou.
♡☐	Fill your bucket with sand, and then flip it over.	バケツにお砂をたくさん入れて、ひっくり返してごらん。 Baketsuni osunawo takusan irete hikkuri kaeshite goran.
♡☐	Pull the bucket straight up.	バケツをまっすぐ持ち上げて。 Baketsuwo massugu mochiagete.
♡☐	You made a sand castle!	砂のお城できたね！ Sunano oshiro dekitane!

B

to burp げっぷ
geppu

I need to burp you. (to a baby) — げっぷしなきゃね。 Geppu shinakyane.

Did I burp you already? — もうげっぷでたかな？ Mou geppu detakana?

Hey. Don't burp in my face. (to a child) — ちょっと。顔に向かってげっぷしないで。 Chotto. Kaoni mukatte geppu shinaide.

Stop burping. — げっぷ、やめて。 Geppu yamete.

the bus バス
basu

We need to go to the bus stop. — バス停に行かなきゃ。 Basuteini ikanakya.

The bus is coming. — バスが来るよ。 Basuga kuruyo.

Get on the bus. — バスに乗って。 Basuni notte.

Get off the bus. — バスから降りて。 Basukara orite.

USE JAPANESE AT HOME

B

♥ ☑
♡ ☐ **Bye!** **バイバイ!**
Baibai!

♡ ☐ Good to see you! 会えてよかった!
Aete yokatta!

♡ ☐ See you tomorrow! また明日!
Mata ashita!

♡ ☐ See you later! また後でね!
Mata atodene!

C

learn it!

♥ ☑ *Got it!*

♡ ☐ **Calm down.** 落ち着いて。
Ochitsuite.

the camera　カメラ
kamera

♡ ☐ Should we take a picture?　写真撮ろうか?
Shashin torouka?

♡ ☐ Let's take a picture.　写真撮ろうよ。
Shashin torouyo.

♡ ☐ Look at the camera!　カメラ見て!
Kamera mite!

USE JAPANESE AT HOME

C

- Looks great! きれいに写ってるね。
  Kireini utsutterune.
- Let's take one more. もう一枚撮ろう。
  Mou ichimai torou.

the car 車
kuruma

- Go to the car. 車のところに行って。
  Kurumano tokoroni itte.
- Get in the car. 車に乗って。
  Kurumani notte.
- Get in your seat. 席に座って。
  Sekini suwatte.
- Get in your car seat. *(child seat)* チャイルドシートに座って。
  Chairudoshiitoni suwatte.
- Get in your seats. 自分の席に座って。
  Jibunno sekini suwatte.
- Get in your car seats. 自分のチャイルドシートに座って。
  Jibunno chairudoshiitoni suwatte.
- Buckle your seat belt(s). シートベルト締めて。
  Shiitoberuto shimete.
- Unbuckle your seat belt(s). シートベルト外して。
  Shiitoberuto hazushite.

C

Everyone out of the car. 　みんな、車から降りて。
Minna kurumakara orite.

Stand next to the car. 　車の横に立って。
Kurumano yokoni tatte.

Stop. A car is coming. 　止まって。車が来るよ。
Tomatte. Kurumaga kuruyo.

the (toy) car 　（おもちゃの）車
(omochano) kuruma

Where is your car? 　車、どこに行っちゃったの？
Kuruma dokoni icchattano?

Play with your cars. 　車で遊んだら。
Kurumade asondara.

Let's play with your cars? 　車で遊ばない？
Kurumade asobanai?

Let's play with your cars. 　車で遊ぼう。
Kurumade asobou.

Here comes the car. 　車が来るよ。
Kurumaga kuruyo.

Vroom. Vroom. 　ぶー、ぶー。
Buu, buu.

You may bring one car with you. 　車、一つだけ持ってきていいよ。
Kuruma hitotsudake mottekite iiyo.

USE JAPANESE AT HOME

C

♥ ☑
♡ ☐ You may take one car with you. 車、一つだけ持って行ってもいいよ。
Kuruma hitotsudake motteittemo iiyo.

♡ ☐ Put your cars away. 車、お片付けして。
Kuruma okatazuke shite.

♡ ☐ **Careful!** 気をつけて!
Kiwo tsukete!

♡ ☐ Pour the water carefully. お水、気をつけて入れてね。
Omizu, kiwo tsukete iretene.

♡ ☐ **Carry me!** 抱っこして!
Dakko shite!

♡ ☐ Do you want me to carry you? 抱っこして欲しい?
Dakko shite hoshii?

♡ ☐ She/He likes to be carried. (Name)は抱っこが大好きなんです。
(Name)wa dakkoga daisuki nandesu.

C

the class 授業
(*school class*) **jugyou**

the lesson 習い事
naraigoto

It's time for your class. 授業の時間だよ。
Jugyouno jikan dayo.

It's time for your lesson. 習い事に行く時間だよ。
Naraigotoni iku jikan dayo.

Go to class now. 今すぐクラスに行って。
Ima sugu kurasuni itte.

Go to your lesson now. 今すぐ習い事に行って。
Imasugu naraigotoni itte.

How was class? 授業どうだった？
Jugyou doudatta?

How was your lesson? 習い事どうだった？
Naraigoto doudatta?

Good. よかったよ。
Yokattayo.

to clean 綺麗にする
kireini suru

Clean the table. テーブル拭いて。
Teeburu fuite.

USE JAPANESE AT HOME

75

C

- ♥ ☑
- ♡ ☐ Let's clean the table before we put the plates on it.
  お皿並べる前に、テーブル拭こうね。
  Osara naraberu maeni teeburu fukoune.
- ♡ ☐ Clean the counter.
  カウンター拭いて。
  Kauntaawo fuite.
- ♡ ☐ Let's clean the counter before we start cooking.
  お料理始める前に、カウンター拭こうね。
  Oryouri hajimeru maeni kauntaa fukoune.
- ♡ ☐ Clean the windows.
  窓を拭いて。
  Madowo fuite.
- ♡ ☐ I cleaned my room already.
  もう部屋の掃除したよ。
  Mou heyano souji shitayo.
- ♡ ☐ I cleaned the whole house today.
  今日は、家中のお掃除したよ。
  Kyouwa iejuuno osouji shitayo.
- ♡ ☐ The house is clean.
  お家、きれいだね。
  Ouchi kireidane.

to clean up 片付ける
katazukeru

- ♡ ☐ We need to clean up.
  片付けなきゃ。
  Katazukenakya.
- ♡ ☐ Time to clean up.
  お片付けの時間だよ。
  Okatazukeno jikan dayo.

C

♥☑			
♡☐	Clean up the table.	テーブルの上片付けて。 Teeburuno ue katazukete.	
♡☐	Please clean up your mess.	自分で散らかしたものは、自分で片付けて。 Jibunde chirakashita monowa jibunde katazukete.	
♡☐	You need to clean your room.	自分の部屋の掃除しなきゃね。 Jibunno heyano souji shinakyane.	
♡☐	Let's clean up your toys together.	一緒におもちゃ片付けよう。 Isshoni omocha katazukeyou.	

> CHORE CARDS AND CHECKLISTS FOR CLEANING UP AT HOME IN THE TALKBOX.MOM SUBSCRIPTION

to close 閉める
shimeru

♡☐	Do you want me to close the door for you?	ドア閉めてほしい？ Doa shimete hoshii?
♡☐	Close the door.	ドア、閉めて。 Doa shimete.
♡☐	Close the cupboard.	食器棚、閉めて。 Shokkidana shimete.
♡☐	Close the box.	箱のフタして。 Hakono futa shite.

USE JAPANESE AT HOME

C

Close the drawer. 引き出し、閉めて。
Hikidashi shimete.

the clothes 服
fuku

Pick up your clothes. 服拾って。
Fuku hirotte.

Let's pick up the clothes. 服拾おう。
Fuku hiroou.

Take your clothes to the laundry room. 服は洗濯機のところに持って行って。
Fukuwa sentakkino tokoroni motteitte.

Let's take the clothes to the laundry room. 服は洗濯機のところに持っていこうね。
Fukuwa sentakkino tokoroni motteikoune.

Hang up the clothes. 服、干して。
Fuku hoshite.

Let's hang up the clothes. 服、干そうね。
Fuku hosoune.

C

the cloud 雲
kumo

Look at the clouds. あの雲見て。
Ano kumo mite.

The clouds are dark. 雲が黒っぽいね。
Kumoga kuroppoine.

It looks like it's going to rain. 雨が降りそうだね。
Amega furisou dane.

Those are rain clouds. あれは、雨雲だね。
Arewa amagumo dane.

cold 冷たい
tsumetai

(weather) 寒い
samui

It's cold. 冷たい。
Tsumetai.

I'm cold. 寒い。
Samui.

I'm freezing. すごく寒い。
Sugoku samui.

USE JAPANESE AT HOME

C

to color 色ぬり
ironuri

Do you want to color?	色、塗りたい？ Iro nuritai?
Go get your crayons and coloring books.	クレヨンとぬりえ取ってきて。 Kureyonto nurie tottekite.
Do you want a piece of paper?	紙、ほしい？ Kami hoshii?
Would you like the yellow crayon?	黄色のクレヨン使う？ Kiirono kureyon tsukau?
Please pass me the black crayon.	黒のクレヨン、貸して。 Kurono kureyon kashite.
Where did the blue crayon go?	青のクレヨン、どこに行っちゃったのかな。 Aono kureyon dokoni icchattanokana.

> LANGUAGE GUIDES, WALL CHARTS & ACTIVITIES FOR ARTS AND CRAFTS IN THE TALKBOX.MOM SUBSCRIPTION

Pass your (*older*) brother the red crayon.	お兄ちゃんに赤のクレヨンを取ってあげて。 Oniichanni akano kureyonwo totte agete.
Pass your (*younger*) brother the red crayon.	弟に赤のクレヨンを取ってあげて。 Otootoni akano kureyonwo totte agete.

C

♥☑		
♡☐	Pass your (*older*) sister the red crayon.	お姉ちゃんに赤のクレヨンを取ってあげて。 Oneechanni akano kureyonwo totte agete.
♡☐	Pass your (*younger*) sister the red crayon.	妹に赤のクレヨンを取ってあげて。 Imoutoni akano kureyonwo totte agete.
♡☐	The white crayon doesn't show on white paper.	白いクレヨンは、白い紙の上で見えないよ。 Shiroi kureyonwa shiroi kamino uede mienaiyo.
♡☐	The pink crayon broke.	ピンクのクレヨンが折れちゃった。 Pinkuno kureyonga orechatta.
♡☐	I can't find the green crayon.	緑のクレヨンが見つからない。 Midorino kureyonga mitsukaranai.
♡☐	Your crayon fell on the floor.	クレヨンが床に落ちたよ。 Kureyonga yukani ochitayo.
♡☐	What a beautiful picture!	わあ、上手に描けたね！ Waa jouzuni kaketane!
♡☐	Put the crayons away.	クレヨン、片付けて。 Kureyon katazukete.
♡☐	Don't color on the wall.	壁に色塗っちゃダメ。 Kabeni iro nuccha dame.
♡☐	Only color on your paper, please.	色塗るのは紙の上だけにしてね。 Iro nurunowa kamino uedakeni shitene.

USE JAPANESE AT HOME

C

to comb 髪をとかす
kamiwo tokasu

Please comb your hair. 髪の毛とかしてね。
Kaminoke tokashitene.

Let's comb your hair. 髪の毛とかそうね。
Kaminoke tokasoune.

to come 来る
kuru

Please come here. こっちに来てください。
Kocchini kite kudasai.

Come here right now. すぐにこっちに来て。
Suguni kocchini kite.

Are you coming? 来ないの？
Konaino?

I'm/We're coming! 今いくよ！
Ima ikuyo!

Come in! 入って！
Haitte!

C

the computer パソコン
pasokon

- Do you want to play a computer game? — パソコンのゲームで遊びたい？ Pasokonno geemude asobitai?
- You've been playing computer games all day. — 一日中パソコンのゲームで遊んでるでしょ。 Ichinichijuu pasokonno geemude asonderudesho.
- I need to use the computer. — パソコン使いたいの。 Pasokon tsukaitaino.
- It's time to get off the computer. — もうパソコン、おしまい。 Mou pasokon oshimai.
- You're grounded from the computer. — パソコン使うの禁止にするよ。 Pasokon tsukauno kinshini suruyo.

to cook 料理する
ryouri suru

- I need to cook dinner. — 夕飯作らなきゃ。 Yuuhan tsukuranakya.
- Do you want to help me cook? — お料理手伝ってくれる？ Oryouri tetsudatte kureru?

USE JAPANESE AT HOME

C

Cool! いいね!
Iine!

to count 数える
kazoeru

Let's count how many ducks there are. アヒルが何羽いるか、数えてみよう。
Ahiruga nanwa iruka kazoete miyou.

I counted 10 ducks. 数えたらアヒルは十羽だったよ。
Kazoetara ahiruwa jippa dattayo.

One. 一羽
Ichiwa.

Two. 二羽
Niwa.

Three. 三羽
Sanwa.

Four. 四羽
Yonwa.

Five. 五羽
Gowa.

Six. 六羽
Roppa.

Seven. 七羽
Nanawa.

C

- Eight. 八羽
  Happa.
- Nine. 九羽
  Kyuuwa.
- Ten. 十羽
  Jippa.

> LEARN TO COUNT, CALCULATE, AND EXPRESS AGE, DATES, & TEMP. IN THE TALKBOX.MOM SUBSCRIPTION

to cry 泣く
naku

- Why are you crying? なんで泣いてるの？
  Nande naiteruno?
- Please stop crying, and tell me what you need. 泣くのやめて、何がほしいのか教えて。
  Nakuno yamete, naniga hoshiinoka oshiete.
- The baby is crying. 赤ちゃんが泣いてる。
  Akachanga naiteru.
- The baby won't stop crying. 赤ちゃんが泣きやまない。
  Akachanga nakiyamanai.

D

learn it!

❤️☑ *Got it!*

	to dance	踊る **odoru**
♡☐	Let's dance?	踊ろうか？ Odorouka?
♡☐	Do you want to dance?	踊りたい？ Odoritai?
♡☐	Do you like to dance?	踊るの好き？ Odoruno suki?
♡☐	I'm a dancer. (*for a male*)	ぼくはダンサーなんだ。 Bokuwa dansaa nanda.
♡☐	(*for a female*)	私はダンサーなの。 Watashiwa dansaa nano.

USE JAPANESE AT HOME

D

dark 暗い
kurai

It's getting dark outside. 外が暗くなって来たよ。
Sotoga kuraku natte kitayo.

It's still dark out. まだ外は暗いよ。
Mada sotowa kuraiyo.

I'm afraid of the dark. 暗いとこ怖い。
Kurai toko kowai.

the diaper オムツ
omutsu

Your diaper stinks. オムツが臭いね。
Omutsuga kusaine.

Time to change your diaper. オムツ替える時間だね。
Omutsu kaeru jikan dane.

We need to change your diaper now. すぐにオムツ替えなきゃ。
Suguni omutsu kaenakya.

Your diaper is full. オムツがパンパンだよ。
Omutsuga panpan dayo.

You pooped in your diaper. オムツでウンチしたね。
Omutsude unchi shitane.

You only peed in your diaper. オムツでおしっこしただけだったね。
Omutsude oshikkoshita dake dattane.

D

♥☑	The diaper is still dry.	まだオムツ濡れてないね。 Mada omutsu nurete naine.
♡☐	Poop went out of the diaper, and down his/her legs.	ウンチがオムツから漏れて、足に垂れて来ちゃってる。 Unchiga omutsukara morete ashini tarete kichatteru.
♡☐	He/She pooped up her back.	背中の方までウンチしちゃってる。 Senakano houmade unchi shichatteru.

> STEP BY STEP LANGUAGE GUIDE FOR CHANGING DIAPERS IN THE TALKBOX.MOM SUBSCRIPTION

the diaper bag オムツ入れ
omutsuire

♡☐	I need to pack the diaper bag.	オムツ入れにオムツ詰めなきゃ。 Omutsuireni omutsu tsumenakya.
♡☐	Did you pull everything out of the diaper bag?	オムツ入れから全部だした？ Omutsuirekara zenbu dashita?
♡☐	Where is the diaper bag?	オムツ入れどこ？ Omutsuire doko?
♡☐	I can't find the diaper bag.	オムツ入れが見つからない。 Omutsuirega mitsukaranai.

USE JAPANESE AT HOME

D

♥ ☑
♡ ☐ Help me find the diaper bag, please. オムツ入れ見つけるの手伝って。
Omutsuire mitsukeruno tetsudatte.

♡ ☐ It's in the diaper bag. オムツ入れの中に入ってるよ。
Omutsuireno nakani haitteruyo.

to dig 掘る
horu

♡ ☐ You can dig in the dirt. 土に穴掘ってもいいよ。
Tsuchini ana hottemo iiyo.

♡ ☐ Do not dig in the yard. お庭で穴掘らないでね。
Oniwade ana horanaidene.

♡ ☐ Dig in the sand. 砂場で穴掘って。
Sunabade ana hotte.

♡ ☐ What are you digging for? 何のために掘ってるの？
Nanno tameni hotteruno?

♡ ☐ Are you digging for treasure? 宝物を掘り当てようとしてるの？
Takaramono horiateyouto shiteruno?

the dirt 泥
doro

♡ ☐ Don't play in the dirt. 泥のところで遊ばないで。
Dorono tokorode asobanaide.

D

There is dirt all over you.
体中泥だらけだよ。
Karadajuu dorodarake dayo.

I don't mind if they play in the dirt.
泥のところで遊んでも構わないよ。
Dorono tokorode asondemo kamawanaiyo.

Kids are supposed to get dirty.
子どもは、泥だらけになるもんだよ。
Kodomowa dorodarakeni narumon dayo.

dirty 汚い
kitanai

Take your shoes off, so you don't get the floor dirty.
床を汚さないように、靴ぬいで。
Yukawo yogosanaiyouni, kutsu nuide.

You're getting the couch dirty. Take your shoes off.
ソファーを汚してるよ。靴ぬいで。
Sofaawo yogoshiteruyo. Kutsu nuide.

Your shirt is really dirty.
シャツが本当に汚いね。
Shatsuga hontouni kitanaine.

How did you get so dirty?
どうやってそんなに汚くなったの？
Douyatte sonnani kitanakunattano?

Did you play in the dirt?
泥のところで遊んだの？
Dorono tokorode asondano?

USE JAPANESE AT HOME

D

♥ ☑
♡ ☐ Your face is dirty.   お顔が汚れてるよ。
                            Okaoga yogoreteruyo.

♡ ☐ Let's wipe it.   拭こうね。
                            Fukoune.

LANGUAGE GUIDES FOR SETTING THE TABLE AND CLEANING UP IN THE TALKBOX.MOM SUBSCRIPTION

---

the dishwasher   食洗機
                      shokusenki

♡ ☐ Everyone load the dishwasher.   みんな、食洗機に入れてね。
                                      Minna, shokusenkini iretene.

♡ ☐ Please put your plate in the dishwasher.   自分の使ったお皿は食洗機に入れてね。
                                                  Jibunno tsukatta osarawa shokusenkini iretene.

♡ ☐ Please put your bowl in the dishwasher.   自分の使ったボウルは食洗機に入れてね。
                                                  Jibunno tsukatta bouruwa shokusenkini iretene.

♡ ☐ Please put your spoon in the dishwasher.   自分の使ったスプーンは食洗機に入れてね。
                                                  Jibunno tsukatta supuunwa shokusenkini iretene.

D

♥☑ ♡☐	Please put your fork in the dishwasher.	自分の使ったフォークは食洗機に入れてね。 Jibunno tsukatta fookuwa shokusenkini iretene.
♡☐	Please put your cup in the dishwasher.	自分の使ったコップは食洗機に入れてね。 Jibunno tsukatta koppuwa shokusenkini iretene.
♡☐	I'm loading the dishwasher.	食洗機に食器入れてるところ。 Shokusenkini shokki ireteru tokoro.
♡☐	I'm about to start the dishwasher.	食洗機、まわすよ。 Shokusenki mawasuyo.
♡☐	I'm unloading the dishwasher.	食洗機から食器出してるところ。 Shokusenkikara shokki dashiteru tokoro.
♡☐	Do you want to help me load the dishwasher?	食洗機に食器入れるのお手伝いする? Shokusenkini shokki ireruno otetsudai suru?
♡☐	Do you want to help me unload the dishwasher?	食洗機から食器出すのお手伝いする? Shokusenki kara shokki dasuno otetsudai suru?
♡☐	The dishwasher is clean.	食洗機のお皿もうきれいだよ。 Shokusenkino osara mou kireidayo.

USE JAPANESE AT HOME

D

- ♥ ☑ / ♡ ☐ The dishwasher is dirty. 食洗機のお皿まだ汚いよ。 Shokusenkino osara mada kitanaiyo.

to do する
suru

- ♡ ☐ You can do it! できるよ！ Dekiruyo!
- ♡ ☐ I knew you could do it. できると思ってたよ。 Dekiruto omottetayo.
- ♡ ☐ I can do it by myself. 自分でできるよ。 Jibunde dekiruyo.
- ♡ ☐ What are you doing? 何してるの？ Nani shiteruno?
- ♡ ☐ I'm going to the bathroom. トイレに行くところ。 Toireni iku tokoro.
- ♡ ☐ I'm making dinner. 夕飯作ってるの。 Yuuhan tsukutteruno.
- ♡ ☐ I'm cleaning up. お掃除してるの。 Osouji shiteruno.
- ♡ ☐ I'm playing. 遊んでるの。 Asonderuno.
- ♡ ☐ I'm watching a show. テレビ観てるの。 Terebi miteruno.

D

the doll お人形
oningyou

♡ ☐	How is your baby doll doing?	お人形は元気にしてるかな？ Oningyouwa genkini shiterukana?
♡ ☐	You are such a good mama.	いいママだね。 Ii mama dane.
♡ ☐	You are such a good daddy.	いいパパだね。 Ii papa dane.
♡ ☐	Is your baby sleeping?	赤ちゃん、寝てるの？ Akachan neteruno?
♡ ☐	My baby is sleeping.	赤ちゃんは寝てる。 Akachanwa neteru.
♡ ☐	My baby is awake.	赤ちゃんは起きてる。 Akachanwa okiteru.
♡ ☐	Are you taking care of your doll?	お人形のお世話してあげてるの？ Oningyouno osewashite ageteruno?
♡ ☐	I'm feeding my baby.	赤ちゃんにごはんあげてるの。 Akachanni gohan ageteruno.
♡ ☐	Where is your doll?	お人形は、どこにあるの？ Oningyouwa dokoni aruno?
♡ ☐	Here is your doll.	はい、お人形、あったよ。 Hai, oningyou attayo.
♡ ☐	Your doll is so pretty.	すごくかわいいお人形だね。 Sugoku kawaii oningyou dane.

D

♥ ☑

	Don't	...ない
		...nai
	(rule)	...だめ
		...dame
	(request)	...ないで
		...naide
	(precaution)	...ないでね
		...naidene

♡ ☐ Don't hit. Be gentle. 叩いちゃダメ。やさしくね。
Tataicha dame. Yasashikune.

♡ ☐ Don't hit me. 叩かないで。
Tatakanaide.

♡ ☐ Don't spit. ツバ吐いちゃダメ。
Tsuba haicha dame.

♡ ☐ Don't spit on me. 私にツバ飛ばさないで。
Watashini tsuba tobasanaide.

♡ ☐ Don't pinch. つねっちゃダメ。
Tsuneccha dame.

♡ ☐ Don't pinch me. つねらないで。
Tsuneranaide.

♡ ☐ Don't scratch. 引っ掻いちゃダメ。
Hikkaicha dame.

♡ ☐ Don't scratch me. 引っ掻かないで。
Hikkakanaide.

♡ ☐ Don't fight. 喧嘩しちゃダメ。
Kenkashicha dame.

D

- ♥☑ Don't throw your toys. Play with your toys nicely. — おもちゃ、投げないの。おもちゃでちゃんと遊んでね。
Omocha nagenaino. Omochade chanto asondene.

- ♡☐ Don't scream in the house. Go outside to play. — 家の中で叫ばないの。外に行って遊んで。
Ieno nakade sakebanaino. Sotoni itte asonde.

- ♡☐ Don't lock your (*older*) brother in the room. — お兄ちゃんを部屋に閉じ込めないの。
Oniichanwo heyani tojikomenaino.

- ♡☐ Don't lock your (*younger*) brother in the room. — 弟を部屋に閉じ込めないの。
Otoutowo heyani tojikomenaino.

- ♡☐ Don't lock your (*older*) sister in the room. — おねえちゃんを部屋に閉じ込めないの。
Oneechanwo heyani tojikomenaino.

- ♡☐ Don't lock your (*younger*) sister in the room. — 妹を部屋に閉じ込めないの。
Imoutowo heyani tojikomenaino.

- ♡☐ Open the door. — ドア、開けて。
Doa akete.

- ♡☐ Don't eat on the couch. — ソファの上で食べないの。
Sofaano uede tabenaino.

- ♡☐ Eat at the table. — テーブルで食べて。
Teeburude tabete.

USE JAPANESE AT HOME

D

♥ ☑

♡ ☐ Don't poke your (*older*) brother.
お兄ちゃんにちょっかい出さないの。
Oniichanni chokkai dasanaino.

♡ ☐ Don't poke your (*younger*) brother.
弟にちょっかい出さないの。
Otoutoni chokkai dasanaino.

♡ ☐ Don't poke your (*older*) sister.
おねえちゃんにちょっかい出さないの。
Oneechanni chokkai dasanaino.

♡ ☐ Don't poke your (*younger*) sister.
妹にちょっかい出さないの。
Imoutoni chokkai dasanaino.

♡ ☐ Don't poke me.
ちょっかい出さないで。
Chokkai dasanaide.

♡ ☐ Don't kick.
蹴っちゃダメ。
Keccha dame.

♡ ☐ Don't kick me.
蹴らないで。
Keranaide.

♡ ☐ Don't touch.
触っちゃダメ。
Sawaccha dame.

♡ ☐ Don't touch me.
触らないで。
Sawaranaide.

♡ ☐ Don't make a mess. Be careful.
ぐちゃぐちゃにしないでね。気をつけて。
Guchaguchani shinaidene. Kiwo tsukete.

D

- ☑ Don't be mean to your friend.
おともだちに意地悪しちゃダメだよ。
Otomodachini ijiwarushicha damedayo.

- ☐ Play nicely.
仲良く遊んでね。
Nakayoku asondene.

- ☐ Don't slam the door. Close it slowly.
ドアをバーンて閉めちゃダメ。ゆっくりそっと閉めて。
Doawo baante shimecha dame. Yukkuri sotto shimete.

- ☐ Don't leave the water running. Turn the water off.
お水出しっぱなしにしちゃダメ。ちゃんと蛇口しめて。
Omizu dashippanashini shicha dame. Chanto jaguchi shimete.

- ☐ Don't wake up the baby.
赤ちゃんを起こさないでね。
Akachanwo okosanaidene.

- ☐ Be very quiet.
静かにね。
Shizukanine.

- ☐ Play in another room.
他の部屋で遊んで。
Hokano heyade asonde.

- ☐ **I don't know.**
わからない。
Wakaranai.

- ☐ I don't know what you are saying.
何言ってるのかわからない。
Nani itterunoka wakaranai.

USE JAPANESE AT HOME

D

I don't know why. なんでだかわかんない。
Nandedaka wakannai.

I don't know the answer. 答えがわかんない。
Kotaega wakannai.

I don't know what happened. 何があったのか知らない。
Naniga attanoka shiranai.

I don't like... **...好きじゃない**
...suki janai

I don't like that toy. そのおもちゃ、好きじゃない。
Sono omocha suki janai.

I don't like to play with cars. 車で遊ぶの、好きじゃない。
Kurumade asobuno suki janai.

I don't like carrots. にんじん、好きじゃない。
Ninjin suki janai.

I don't want... (something) **...ほしくない**
...hoshikunai

I don't want... (to do something) **...したくない**
...shitakunai

I don't need... (something) **...いらない**
...iranai

TALKBOX.MOM

D

I don't want this doll. この人形、ほしくない。
Kono ningyou hoshikunai.

I want the other one. 他のやつがいい。
Hokano yatsuga ii.

You don't want to play right now? 今遊びたくないの？
Ima asobitaku naino?

I don't want to go to school. 学校行きたくない。
Gakkou ikitaku nai.

the door ドア
doa

Push the door. ドア、押して。
Doa oshite.

Pull the door. ドア、引いて。
Doa hiite.

Please open the door. ドア、開けてね。
Doa, aketene.

Please close the door. ドア、閉めてね。
Doa, shimetene.

Please keep the door open. ドア、開けっぱなしにしてて。
Doa akeppanashini shitete.

Knock on the door. ドア、ノックして。
Doa nokkushite.

D

♥ ☑

	the doorbell	インターホン **intaahon**
	(for pre-school children)	ピンポン **pinpon**
♡ ☐	Please ring the doorbell.	インターホン鳴らして。 Intaahon narashite.
♡ ☐ (to a pre-school children)		ピンポン鳴らして。 Pinpon narashite.
♡ ☐	Just one time.	一回だけね。 Ikkai dakene.
♡ ☐	Don't keep ringing the doorbell.	インターホン何回も鳴らさないの。 Intaahon nankaimo narasanaino.
♡ ☐ (to a pre-school children)		ピンポン何回も鳴らさないの。 Pinpon nankaimo narasanaino.

	down	下 **shita**
	(when used as a verb)	下ろす **orosu**
♡ ☐	Do you want me to put you down? (when holding a toddler)	下りたい? Oritai?
♡ ☐	Please put me down.	下ろして。 Oroshite.

D

- ☑ I'll put you down on the couch. — ソファに下ろすね。 Sofaani orosune.
- ☐ I'll put you down on the blanket. — お布団に下ろすね。 Ofutonni orosune.
- ☐ I'll put you down on the grass. — 芝生に下ろすね。 Shibafuni orosune.

downstairs 下
shita

(full word) 下の階
shitano kai

- ☐ Your friends are downstairs. — おともだちは下にいるよ。 Otomodachiwa shitani iruyo.
- ☐ *(also)* おともだちは下の階にいるよ。 Otomodachiwa shitano kaini iruyo.
- ☐ Come downstairs to eat. — 下に来て、食べて。 Shitani kite tabete.

> GET LABEL CARDS FOR ROOMS AND AREAS IN YOUR HOME IN THE TALKBOX.MOM SUBSCRIPTION

- ☐ Go downstairs, and get your blanket. — 下に行って、毛布取ってきて。 Shitani itte moufu tottekite.
- ☐ Go downstairs, and get your glasses. — 下に行って、メガネ取ってきて。 Shitani itte megane tottekite.

USE JAPANESE AT HOME

D

Go downstairs, and get your book. 下に行って、本取ってきて。
Shitani itte hon tottekite.

to draw 描く
kaku

Do you want to draw? お絵かきする？
Oekaki suru?

What are you drawing? 何描いてるの？
Nani kaiteruno?

I'm drawing a dog. 犬描いてるの。
Inu kaiteruno.

I'm drawing a dragon. ドラゴン描いてるの。
Doragon kaiteruno.

I'm drawing a princess. お姫様描いてるの。
Ohimesama kaiteruno.

I'm drawing a dinosaur. 恐竜描いてるの。
Kyouryuu kaiteruno.

I'm drawing a house. お家描いてるの。
Ouchi kaiteruno.

I drew a picture of my family. 家族の絵描いたよ。
Kazokuno e kaitayo.

This is daddy. これがパパ。
Korega papa.

D

- ♥ ☑ This is mommy. これがママ。
  Korega mama.
- ♡ ☐ This is me. これが私。
  (for a female) Korega watashi.
- ♡ ☐ *(for a male)* これがぼく。
  Korega boku.
- ♡ ☐ Thank you for 絵、描いてくれてありがとう！
  drawing me a picture! E kaitekurete arigatou.

> LANGUAGE GUIDES, WALL CHARTS & ACTIVITIES FOR ARTS AND CRAFTS IN THE TALKBOX.MOM SUBSCRIPTION

to get dressed 着替える
kigaeru

- ♡ ☐ Please get dressed. お着替えして。
  Okigae shite.
- ♡ ☐ You need to get 着替えなきゃね。
  dressed. Kigaenakyane.
- ♡ ☐ Do you want me to お着替え手伝って欲しい？
  help you get dressed? Okigae tesudatte hoshii?

> CLOTHING CHART & STEP BY STEP GUIDES FOR DRESSING CHILDREN IN THE TALKBOX.MOM SUBSCRIPTION

USE JAPANESE AT HOME

D

to drink 飲む
nomu

Drink your water, please. お水飲んで。
Omizu nonde.

You drank all of your juice. *(just now)* ジュース全部飲んだね。
Juusu zenbu nondane.

(in the past, like yesterday) ジュースは、全部飲んじゃったでしょ。
Juusuwa zenbu nonjatta desho.

GET LANGUAGE GUIDES FOR DRINKS AND SPILLING DRINKS IN THE TALKBOX.MOM SUBSCRIPTION

---

to drop 落とす
otosu

You dropped your toy. おもちゃ落としたよ。
Omocha otoshitayo.

I dropped the binky on the ground. おしゃぶり地面に落としちゃった。
Oshaburi jimenni otoshichatta.

(to a baby or toddler) おしゃぶり下に落としちゃった。
Oshaburi shitani otoshichatta.

Drop what you are holding. 手に持ってるもの捨てて。
Teni motteru mono sutete.

You dropped your binky. おしゃぶり落としたよ。
Oshaburi otoshitayo.

TALKBOX.MOM

D

♥☑		
♡☐	You dropped your wallet.	お財布落としたよ。 Osaifu otoshitayo.
♡☐	You dropped your paper.	紙、落としたよ。 Kami otoshitayo.
♡☐	Did you drop your binky?	おしゃぶり落としちゃったの？ Oshaburi otoshichattano?
♡☐	Did you drop your wallet?	お財布落としちゃったの？ Osaifu otoshichattano?
♡☐	Did you drop your paper?	紙、落としちゃったの？ Kami otoshichattano?
♡☐	You are going to drop your binky.	おしゃぶり落としちゃうよ。 Oshaburi otoshichauyo.

	the drum	太鼓 **taiko**
♡☐	Play your drum!	太鼓叩いて！ Taiko tataite!
♡☐	Can you tap on the drum with the stick?	太鼓、棒で叩ける？ Taiko boude tatakeru?

USE JAPANESE AT HOME

D

dry 乾いている
kawaiteiru

to dry 乾かす
kawakasu

to dry off 拭く
fuku

The clothes are dry. 洋服、乾いてるよ。
Youfuku kawaiteruyo.

Let's dry you off. 体、拭こうね。
Karada fukoune.

Let me dry your face. 顔、拭いてあげる。
Kao, fuite ageru.

the dryer 乾燥機
kansouki

Help me move the clothes to the dryer. 服、乾燥機に入れるの手伝って。
Fuku kansoukini ireruno tetsudatte.

The clothes are still in the dryer. 服は、まだ乾燥機の中にあるよ。
Fukuwa mada kansoukino nakani aruyo.

Did you move the clothes to the dryer? 服、乾燥機に入れた？
Fuku kansoukini ireta?

E

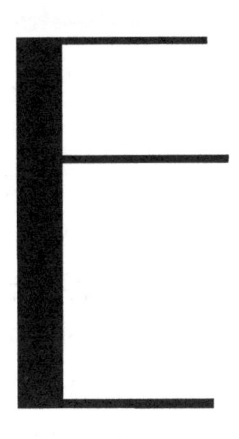

learn it!

♥☑ *Got it!*

to eat 食べる
taberu

♡☐ What would you like to eat? 　何食べたい?
　Nani tabetai?

♡☐ He/She didn't eat all of his/her dinner. 　(Name) 夕飯残したよ。
　(Name) yuuhan nokoshitayo.

♡☐ Let me finish eating. 　食べ終わるまで待ってて。
　Tabeowaru made mattete.

> LANGUAGE GUIDES FOR SNACKS, DRINKS, MEALS, AND DINING IN THE TALKBOX.MOM SUBSCRIPTION

USE JAPANESE AT HOME

E

the elevator エレベーター
erebeetaa

Who wants to push the button? ボタン押したい人？
Botan oshitai hito?

I want to push the button! *(for a male)* ぼくが押したい！
Bokuga oshitai!

(for a female) 私が押したい！
Watashiga oshitai!

(Name) gets to push the button. (Name)がボタン押す係ね。
(Name)ga botan osu kakarine.

Push up. 上を押して。
Uewo oshite.

Push down. 下を押して。
Shitawo oshite.

Go in the elevator. エレベーターに乗って。
Erebeetaani notte.

Push the button. ボタンを押して。
Botanwo oshite.

Push this button. このボタンを押して。
Kono botanwo oshite.

Push one. 一階を押して。
Ikkaiwo oshite.

Push two. 二階を押して。
Nikaiwo oshite.

Push three. 三階を押して。
Sankaiwo oshite.

TALKBOX.MOM

E

♥☑			
♡☐	Push four.	四階を押して。 Yonkaiwo oshite.	
♡☐	Push five.	五階を押して。 Gokaiwo oshite.	
♡☐	Push six.	六階を押して。 Rokkaiwo oshite.	
♡☐	Push seven.	七階を押して。 Nanakaiwo oshite.	
♡☐	This is not our floor. Stay in.	この階じゃないよ。まだ降りないで。 Kono kaija naiyo. Mada orinaide.	
♡☐	We're here. Go on out.	ついたよ。降りて。 Tsuitayo. Orite.	

	emotions	気持ち **kimochi**
♡☐	How are you feeling?	気分はどう？ Kibunwa dou?
♡☐	Better.	少し良くなった。 Sukoshi yokunatta.
♡☐	About the same.	あまり変わらない。 Amari kawaranai.
♡☐	Worse.	悪くなった。 Warukunatta.

USE JAPANESE AT HOME

E

♥☑			
♡☐	I'm excited.	ワクワクする。	Wakuwaku suru.
♡☐	I'm grumpy.	嫌な気持ち。	Iyana kimochi.
♡☐	I'm happy.	嬉しい。	Ureshii.
♡☐	I'm mad.	怒ってる。	Okotteru.
♡☐	I'm very mad.	すごく怒ってる。	Sugoku okotteru.
♡☐	I'm nervous.	緊張してる。	Kinchou shiteru.
♡☐	I'm stressed.	ストレスたまってる。	Sutoresu tamatteru.
♡☐	I'm scared.	怖い。	Kowai.
♡☐	**Excuse me.**	**すみません。**	**Sumimasen.**
♡☐	Excuse me. May I go by please?	すみません。通ってもいいですか？	Sumimasen. Toottemo iidesuka?
♡☐	Excuse me. Do you know what time it is?	すみません。今何時かわかりますか？	Sumimasen. Ima nanjika wakarimasuka?

E

♥ ☑
♡ ☐ Excuse me. *(when you bump into someone)* すみません。
Sumimasen.

to exercise 運動する
undou suru

♡ ☐ I need to exercise more. もっと運動しなきゃ。
Motto undou shinakya.

♡ ☐ I'm going to exercise. 運動するの。
Undou suruno.

♡ ☐ I'm going to the gym. ジムに行くの。
Jimuni ikuno.

♡ ☐ Do you want to exercise with me? 一緒に運動したい？
Isshoni undou shitai?

♡ ☐ Daddy is exercising. パパは運動してるよ。
Papawa undou shiteruyo.

♡ ☐ Mommy is exercising. ママは運動してるよ。
Mamawa undou shiteruyo.

> ACTION CHART FOR MOVING + EXERCISING IN THE TALKBOX.MOM SUBSCRIPTION

USE JAPANESE AT HOME

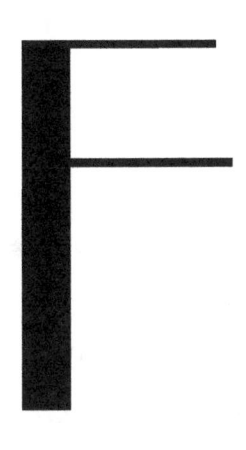

F

learn it!

♥☑ *Got it!*

	fall off	落ちる **ochiru**
	trip over	転ぶ **korobu**
♥☐	I don't want you to climb up there. You could fall off.	そこに登って欲しくないな。落ちるよ。 Sokoni nobotte hoshiku naina. Ochiruyo.
♥☐	I fell off.	落ちちゃった。 Ochichatta.
♥☐	I tripped over.	転んじゃった。 Koronjatta.
♥☐	You fell off.	落ちちゃったね。 Ochichattane.

USE JAPANESE AT HOME

F

You tripped over. 転んじゃったね。
Koronjattane.

to fart おならをする
onarawo suru

Did you just fart? 今おならした？
Ima onara shita?

Who farted? おならしたの誰？
Onara shitano dare?

Someone farted. 誰かおならしたでしょ。
Dareka onara shitadesho.

I farted! *(for a male)* ぼくがおならした！
Bokuga onara shita!

(for a female) 私がおならした！
Watashiga onara shita!

Gross! やめてよ。
Yameteyo!

Fast! 速く！
Hayaku!

Faster. もっと速く。
Motto hayaku.

F

♥ ☑
♡ ☐ You run really fast. 走るのがすごく速いね。
Hashirunoga sugoku hayaine.

favorite 好きな
sukina

♡ ☐ What is your favorite toy? お気に入りのおもちゃは何？
Okiniirino omochawa nani?

♡ ☐ Which is your favorite (toy) car? お気に入りの車はどれ？
Okiniirino kurumawa dore?

♡ ☐ This is my favorite picture. (a photo) (for a female) これが私の好きな写真だよ。
Korega watashino sukina shashindayo.

♡ ☐ (for a male) これがぼくの好きな写真だよ。
Korega bokuno sukina shashindayo.

♡ ☐ This is my favorite picture. (an illustration) (for a female) これが私の好きなイラストだよ。
Korega watashino sukina irasutodayo.

♡ ☐ (for a male) これがぼくの好きなイラストだよ。
Korega bokuno sukina irasutodayo.

♡ ☐ This is my favorite picture. (a painting) (for a female) これが私の好きな絵だよ。
Korega watashino sukina edayo.

USE JAPANESE AT HOME

F

(for a male) これがぼくの好きな絵だよ。
Korega bokuno sukina edayo.

to finish 終える
oeru

Are you finished? 終わったの？
Owattano?

I am finished. 終わったよ。
Owattayo.

to fix 直す
naosu

Please fix my toy. It broke. *(for a female)* 私のおもちゃ直して。壊れちゃった。
Watashino omocha naoshite. Kowarechatta.

(for a male) ぼくのおもちゃ直して。壊れちゃった。
Bokuno omocha naoshite. Kowarechatta.

Let me fix your toy. おもちゃ、直してあげるね。
Omocha naoshite agerune.

I will fix your toy. おもちゃ直すからね。
Omocha naosu karane.

F

Your toy cannot be fixed. — このおもちゃは直せないよ。
Kono omochawa naosenaiyo.

the flower 花
hana

Look at those beautiful flowers. — あの綺麗なお花見て。
Ano kireina ohana mite.

Would you like to water the flowers? — お花にお水あげたい？
Ohanani omizu agetai?

Let's water the flowers. — お花にお水あげようね。
Ohanani omizu ageyoune

I'm watering the flowers. — お花にお水をあげてるんだよ。
Ohanani omizuwo ageterundayo.

> LANGUAGE GUIDES FOR SNACKS, DRINKS, MEALS, AND DINING IN THE TALKBOX.MOM SUBSCRIPTION

the food 食べ物
tabemono

Eat all of your food. — 残さず全部食べてね。
Nokosazu zenbu tabetene.

Don't play with your food. — 食べ物で遊ばないの。
Tabemonode asobanaino.

USE JAPANESE AT HOME

F

♥ ☑	**to forget**	忘れる **wasureru**
♡ ☐	I forgot my wallet.	お財布忘れてきちゃった。 Osaifu wasurete kichatta.
♡ ☐	I forgot my bag.	カバン忘れてきちゃった。 Kaban wasurete kichatta.
♡ ☐	I forgot my school bag.	学校のカバン忘れてきちゃった。 Gakkouno kaban wasurete kichatta.
♡ ☐	I forgot my backpack. *(for school)*	ランドセル忘れてきちゃった。 Randoseru wasurete kichatta.
♡ ☐	I forgot my homework.	宿題忘れてきちゃった。 Shukudai wasurete kichatta.
♡ ☐	I forgot my phone.	ケータイ忘れてきちゃった。 Keetai wasurete kichatta.
♡ ☐	Sorry. I forgot.	ごめんなさい。忘れました。 Gomennasai. Wasuremashita.
♡ ☐	I forgot what I was going to say.	何を言おうとしていたのか忘れちゃった。 Naniwo iouto shiteitanoka wasurechatta.
♡ ☐	I forgot why I came in this room.	なんでこの部屋に来たのか忘れちゃった。 Nande kono heyani kitanoka wasurechatta.

F

♥ ☑

the fruit 果物
kudamono

♡ ☐ Do you want some fruit? 果物食べたい?
Kudamono tabetai?

> LANGUAGE GUIDES FOR FRUITS AND PUTTING AWAY FOOD IN THE TALKBOX.MOM SUBSCRIPTION

fun 楽しい
tanoshii

♡ ☐ Are you having fun? 楽しんでる?
Tanoshinderu?

♡ ☐ Did you have fun? 楽しかった?
Tanoshikatta?

♡ ☐ I'm having fun. 楽しいよ。
Tanoshiiyo.

♡ ☐ I'm having so much fun with you. (Name)といると楽しい。
(Name)to iruto tanoshii.

♡ ☐ You are so much fun. (Name)ってすごく楽しいね。
(Name)tte sugoku tanoshiine.

♡ ☐ Playing at your house was so fun. (Name)のお家で遊んだのが楽しかった。
(Name)no ouchide asondanoga tanoshikatta.

USE JAPANESE AT HOME

F

♥ ☑
♡ ☐ Thank you! ありがとう!
Arigatou!

funny 面白い
omoshiroi

♡ ☐ That was funny. それ面白かったよ。
Sore omoshirokattayo.

♡ ☐ You're so funny. (Name)ってすごく面白い。
(Name)tte sugoku omoshiroi.

G

learn it!

♥ ☑ *Got it!*

	the game	**ゲーム**
		geemu
♡ ☐	Let's play a game?	ゲームしない？
		Geemu shinai?
♡ ☐	Let's play a game.	ゲームしよう。
		Geemu shiyou.
♡ ☐	Would you please get out a game?	ゲームやめてくれない？
		Geemu yamete kurenai?
♡ ☐	This is my favorite game.	このゲーム、気に入ってるんだ。
		Kono geemu kiniitterunda.
♡ ☐	Want to play another game?	他のゲームもやってみたい？
		Hokano geemumo yattemitai?

USE JAPANESE AT HOME

G

- Let's play another game.
  他のゲームもやろうよ。
  Hokano geemumo yarouyo.

- We need to put this game away first.
  まずこのゲームを片付けなきゃ。
  Mazu kono geemuwo katazukenakya.

- Put all the pieces back in the box.
  箱の中に全部片付けて。
  Hakono nakani zenbu katazukete.

the gate 門
mon

- The gate is locked.
  門の鍵が閉まってる。
  Monno kagiga shimatteru.

- They can't get in.
  入れないよ。
  Hairenaiyo.

- They can't get out.
  出られないよ。
  Derarenaiyo.

- The gate is open.
  門が開いてる。
  Monga aiteru.

G

the baby gate ベビーゲート
bebiigeeto

Who left the baby gate open? 誰がベビーゲート開けっ放しにしたの？
Darega bebiigeeto akeppanashini shitano?

Shut the baby gate. ベビーゲート閉めて。
Bebiigeeto shimete.

Gently. 優しくね。
Yasashikune.

Be very gentle with the baby. 赤ちゃんにとても優しくしてね。
Akachanni totemo yasashiku shitene.

Be very gentle with the cat. 猫にとても優しくしてね。
Nekoni totemo yasashiku shitene.

Be very gentle with the dog. 犬にとても優しくしてね。
Inuni totemo yasashiku shitene.

to give あげる
ageru

Please give me the toy. おもちゃ、ちょうだい。
Omocha choudai.

G

♥ ☑
♡ ☐ Please give your (*older*) brother the toy. — お兄ちゃんにおもちゃあげて。 Oniichanni omocha agete.

♡ ☐ Please give your (*younger*) brother the toy. — 弟におもちゃあげて。 Otoutoni omocha agete.

♡ ☐ Please give your (*older*) sister the toy. — お姉ちゃんにおもちゃあげて。 Oneechanni omocha agete.

♡ ☐ Please give your (*younger*) sister the toy. — 妹におもちゃあげて。 Imoutoni omocha agete.

♡ ☐ Will you please give my toy back? — おもちゃ返してくれない？ Omocha kaeshite kurenai?

♡ ☐ You need to give him/her the toy back. — おもちゃ、返してあげなきゃダメでしょ。 Omocha kaeshite agenakya damedesho.

LANGUAGE GUIDES, WALL CHARTS & ACTIVITIES FOR ARTS AND CRAFTS IN THE TALKBOX.MOM SUBSCRIPTION

---

the glue のり
nori

♡ ☐ Just use a little bit of glue. — のりは、ちょっとだけつけてね。 Noriwa chottodake tsuketene.

G

That is too much glue. のり、つけすぎだよ。
Nori tsukesugidayo.

Put the glue on your paper. 紙にのりをつけて。
Kamini noriwo tsukete.

Do not eat the glue. のり、食べちゃダメだよ。
Nori tabecha damedayo.

Go! 行くよ！
ikuyo!

Ready! Set! Go! 位置について、よーい、どん！
Ichini tsuite yooi don!

Go away. あっちいって。
Acchi itte.

Let's go. 行こう。
Ikou.

Go by. 通り過ぎて。
Toorisugite.

It's time to go. 行く時間だよ。
Iku jikandayo.

It's about time to go. そろそろいく時間だよ。
Sorosoro iku jikandayo.

It's about time to leave. そろそろ帰る時間だよ。
Sorosoro kaeru jikandayo.

USE JAPANESE AT HOME

G

♥ ☑			
♡ ☐	It's time to leave.	帰る時間だよ。 Kaeru jikandayo.	
♡ ☐	We need to go to school.	学校に行かなきゃ。 Gakkouni ikanakya.	
♡ ☐	We are going to school.	学校に行くよ。 Gakkouni ikuyo.	
♡ ☐	We need to go to the store.	お店に行かなきゃ。 Omiseni ikanakya.	
♡ ☐	I need to go to the store.	お店に行かなきゃ。 Omiseni ikanakya.	
♡ ☐	We need to go to the grocery store.	スーパーに行かなきゃ。 Suupaani ikanakya.	
♡ ☐	We are going to the grocery store.	スーパーに行くの。 Supaani ikuno.	
♡ ☐	I need to go to the post office.	郵便局に行かなきゃ。 Yuubinkyokuni ikanakya.	
♡ ☐	We are going to the post office.	郵便局に行くの。 Yuubinkyokuni ikuno.	
♡ ☐	We are going to get ice cream.	アイスクリーム買いに行くの。 Aisukuriimu kaini ikuno.	
♡ ☐	We need to go to the doctor's office.	お医者さんに行かなきゃ。 Oishasanni ikanakya.	
♡ ☐	We are going to the doctor's office.	お医者さんに行くの。 Oishasanni ikuno.	

G

♥☑		
♡☐	We need to go to the dentist's office.	歯医者さんに行かなきゃ。 Haishasanni ikanakya.
♡☐	We are going to the park.	公園に行くの。 Koenni ikuno.
♡☐	We are going to church.	教会に行くの。 Kyokaini ikuno.
♡☐	We are going to a restaurant.	レストランに行くの。 Resutoranni ikuno.
♡☐	We need to go run errands.	用事を済ませに行かなきゃ。 Youjiwo sumaseni ikanakya.

> ILLUSTRATED CHART FOR ERRANDS & SCHEDULING YOUR CALENDAR IN THE TALKBOX.MOM SUBSCRIPTION

♡☐	**Good job!**	上手！ **Jouzu!**
♡☐	*(You did well!)*	じょうずにできたね！ **Jouzuni dekitane!**
♡☐	*(You did your best!)*	がんばったね！ **Ganbattane!**
♡☐	Fantastic!	すごくいいね！ Sugoku iine!

USE JAPANESE AT HOME

G

the grass (*in a field*) 草
kusa

(*on a lawn*) 芝生
shibafu

Come sit on the grass. (*in a field*)	こっちに来て、草の上に座ろうよ。 Kocchini kite, kusano ueni suwarouyo.
(*on a lawn*)	こっちに来て、芝生に座ろう。 Kocchini kite shibafuni suwarou.
The grass is so green. (*in a field*)	草がきれいな緑色だね。 Kusaga kireina midoriiro dane.
(*on a lawn*)	芝生がきれいな緑色だね。 Shibafuga kireina midoriiro dane.

to grow 大きくなる
ookiku naru

The plant is growing really fast.	植物、大きくなるのはやいね。 Shokubutsu ookikunaruno hayaine.
The tomatoes are growing.	トマトが大きくなってきたね。 Tomatoga ookiku natte kitane.
You have grown so much!	大きくなったね! Ookiku nattane!

G

Eat your vegetables, so you can grow.

もっとお野菜食べれば、大きくなれるよ。

Motto oyasai tabereba ookiku nareruyo.

H

learn it!

♥ ☑ *Got it!*

the hair 髪の毛
kaminoke

♡ ☐ Your hair looks great. 素敵な髪型だね。
Sutekina kamigatadane.

♡ ☐ Your hair is all tangled. 髪の毛ぐちゃぐちゃに絡まってるよ。
Kaminoke guchaguchani karamatteruyo.

♡ ☐ Did you brush your hair? 髪の毛とかした？
Kaminoke tokashita?

♡ ☐ Let's braid your hair. 三つ編みしようね。
Mitsuami shiyoune.

♡ ☐ Let's put your hair up. 髪の毛、上で結ぼうね。
Kaminoke uede musuboune.

USE JAPANESE AT HOME

H

♥ ☑
♡ ☐ Let's put your hair up in a pony tail. ポニーテールにしようね。
Poniiteeruni shiyoune.

to happen 起こる
okoru

♡ ☐ What happened? 何があったの？
Naniga attano?

♡ ☐ What is going on? どうしたの？
Doushitano?

♡ ☐ Nothing. 別に何も。
Betsuni nanimo.

to hate 嫌い
kirai

♡ ☐ I hate broccoli. ブロッコリー嫌い。
Burokkorii kirai.

♡ ☐ I hate going to bed. 寝るの嫌い。
Neruno kirai.

H

the headphones ヘッドフォン
heddofon

the earbuds イヤホン
iyahon

Please use your headphones. ヘッドフォン使ってね。
Heddofon tsukattene.

Where are your headphones? ヘッドフォン、どこ？
Heddofon doko?

Where are your earbuds? イヤホン、どこ？
Iyahon doko?

to hear 聞く
kiku

Do you hear that? 聞こえる？
Kikoeru?

Did you hear that? 聞こえた？
Kikoeta?

I heard a noise. なんか音が聞こえたよ。
Nanka otoga kikoetayo.

Me too. *(for a female)* 私も。
Watashimo.

(for a male) ぼくも。
Bokumo.

USE JAPANESE AT HOME

H

Let's go see what it was. 何の音だったのか、見に行ってみよう。
Nanno otodattanoka mini ittemiyou.

It was a car. 車の音だったよ。
Kurumano otodattayo.

It was a plane. 飛行機の音だったよ。
Hikoukino otodattayo.

the helicopter ヘリコプター
herikoputaa

Fly your helicopter over here. ヘリコプターはこっちで飛ばそう。
Herikoputaawa kocchide tobasou.

Your helicopter is going to crash. ヘリコプター、墜落しちゃうよ。
Herikoputaa tsuiraku shichauyo.

I stepped on your helicopter. ヘリコプター踏んじゃった。
Herikoputaa funjatta.

Don't leave it on the floor. 床に置きっぱなしにしないで。
Yukani okippanashini shinaide.

H

♥ ☑		**Hello!**	**こんにちは！**
			Konnichiwa!
♡ ☐		Good morning!	おはよう！
			Ohayou!
♡ ☐		Good afternoon!	こんにちは！
			Konnichiwa!
♡ ☐		Good evening!	こんばんは！
			Konbanwa!
♡ ☐		Good night!	おやすみなさい！
			Oyasuminasai!

		hot	**あつい**
			atsui
♡ ☐		It's hot.	あついね。
			Atsuine.
♡ ☐		I'm hot.	あつい。
			Atsui.
♡ ☐		You're so sweaty.	汗びっしょりだね。
			Ase bisshoridane.

> LANGUAGE GUIDE FOR DESCRIBING AND DRESSING FOR THE WEATHER IN THE TALKBOX.MOM SUBSCRIPTION

USE JAPANESE AT HOME

H

How are you? 元気？
Genki?

How was work today? お仕事どうだった？
Oshigoto doudatta?

How was school? 学校どうだった？
Gakkou doudatta?

How is your day going? うまくいってる？
Umaku itteru?

How was church? 教会はどうだった？
Kyoukaiwa doudatta?

How is your mom? お母さん、元気？
Okaasan genki?

How is your dad? お父さん、元気？
Otousan genki?

How is your friend doing? お友達は、元気にしてる？
Otomodachiwa genkini shiteru?

Fine. 元気だよ。
Genkidayo.

Having a hard day. 今日は大変な1日だ。
Kyouwa taihenna ichinichida.

My kids have been really good today. 今日は、子どもたちいい子にしてるよ。
Kyouwa kodomotachi iikoni shiteruyo.

My kids have been terrible today. 今日は、子どもたち荒れてる。
Kyouwa kodomotachi areteru.

TALKBOX.MOM

H

♥ ☑		
♡ ☐	So tired. I got woken up a lot last night.	すごく疲れてる。昨日の夜、何度も起こされちゃって。 Sugoku tsukareteru. Kinouno yoru, nandomo okosarechatte.
♡ ☐	Really busy.	本当に忙しい。 Hontouni isogashii.
♡ ☐	Are you okay?	大丈夫？ Daijoubu?
♡ ☐	I'm okay.	大丈夫。 Daijoubu.

> GUIDE + ACTIVITY FOR INTRODUCING YOURSELF & MEETING OTHERS IN THE TALKBOX.MOM SUBSCRIPTION

	hungry	お腹がすく **onakaga suku**
♡ ☐	Are you hungry?	お腹、空いた？ Onaka suita?
♡ ☐	I'm hungry.	お腹すいた。 Onaka suita.
♡ ☐	He/She's acting like that because he's hungry.	(Name)はお腹が空いてるから、そうなっちゃてるんだよ。 (Name)wa onakaga suiterukara sou nacchatterundayo.

USE JAPANESE AT HOME

H

Hurry. 急いで。
Isoide.

to hurt 痛い
itai

Stop! That hurts! やめて！それ痛い！
Yamete! Sore itai!

What hurts? どこが痛いの？
Dokoga itaino?

My... hurts. ....が痛い。
...ga itai.

My head hurts. 頭が痛い。
Atamaga itai.

My arm hurts. 腕が痛い。
Udega itai.

My arms hurt. 両腕が痛い。
Ryouudega itai.

My back hurts. 背中が痛い。
Senakaga itai.

My leg hurts. 脚が痛い。
Ashiga itai.

My legs hurt. 両脚が痛い。
Ryouashiga itai.

H

My foot hurts. 足が痛い。
Ashiga itai.

My feet hurt. 両足が痛い。
Ryouashiga itai.

My eye hurts. 目が痛い。
Mega itai.

My eyes hurt. 両目が痛い。
Ryoumega itai.

My nose hurts. 鼻が痛い。
Hanaga itai.

My mouth hurts. 口が痛い。
Kuchiga itai.

My knee hurts. 膝が痛い。
Hizaga itai.

My knees hurt. 両膝が痛い。
Ryouhizaga itai.

My stomach hurts. お腹が痛い。
Onakaga itai.

to get hurt 怪我をする
kegawo suru

Did you get hurt? 怪我しなかった？
Kega shinakatta?

H

I got hurt. 怪我しちゃった。
Kega shichatta.

I

learn it!

♥ ☑ *Got it!*

		to itch	かゆい **kayui**
♡ ☐		My... itches.	....がかゆい ....ga kayui.
♡ ☐		My back itches.	背中がかゆい。 Senakaga kayui.
♡ ☐		My nose itches.	鼻がかゆい。 Hanaga kayui.
♡ ☐		My leg itches.	脚がかゆい。 Ashiga kayui.

USE JAPANESE AT HOME

I

Don't scratch your leg. Let's put cream on it.

脚、掻いちゃダメ。かゆみ止めクリーム塗ろうね。

Ashi kaicha dame. Kayumidome kuriimu nuroune.

J

learn it!

♥ ☑ *Got it!*

the juice ジュース
juusu

♡ ☐ I want some juice, please. — ジュースください。
Juusu kudasai.

♡ ☐ Water the juice down a little bit without him/her seeing. — 見つからないうちに、ジュースをお水でちょっと薄めちゃおう。
Mitsukaranai uchini juusuwo omizude chotto usumechaou.

> GET LANGUAGE GUIDE FOR DRINKS AND SPILLING DRINKS IN THE TALKBOX.MOM SUBSCRIPTION

USE JAPANESE AT HOME

J

Jump! **ジャンプして!**
Janpu shite!

Don't jump on the bed. ベッドの上で飛び跳ねちゃダメ。
Beddono uede tobihanecha dame.

Let's jump on the trampoline. トランポリンでジャンプしよう。
Toranporinde janpu shiyou.

K

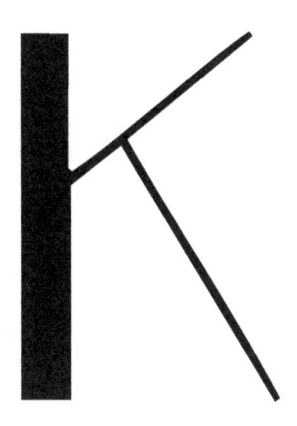

learn it!

♥ ☑ *Got it!*

		the key	鍵 **kagi**
♡ ☐	Where are my keys?	鍵どこにいっちゃったかな。 Kagi dokoni icchattakana.
♡ ☐	Have you seen my keys? *(for a female)*	私の鍵、見かけなかった？ Watashino kagi mikakenakatta?
♡ ☐	*(for a male)*	ぼくの鍵、見かけなかった？ Bokuno kagi mikakenakatta?
♡ ☐	The baby likes to play with keys.	赤ちゃんって鍵で遊ぶの好きだよね。 Akachantte kagide asobuno sukidayone.

USE JAPANESE AT HOME

K

the kiss キス
kisu

(also) チュー
chuu

Kisses! キスよ!
Kisu yo!

Mom, don't kiss me. ママ、チューしないで。
Mama chuu shinaide.

Give me a kiss. チューして。
Chuu shite.

Our baby gives the wettest kisses. 赤ちゃんってベトベトのキスしてくれるよね。
Akachantte betobetono kisu shitekureruyone.

LABEL CARDS FOR HOW TO USE COMMON ITEMS IN THE KITCHEN IN THE TALKBOX.MOM SUBSCRIPTION

---

the kitchen 台所
daidokoro

I'm in the kitchen! 台所にいるよ!
Daidokoroni iruyo!

Get out of the kitchen. 台所から出て行って。
Daidokorokara dete itte.

K

♥ ☑ ♡ ☐	Who made this mess in the kitchen?	台所散らかしたの誰？ Daidokoro chirakashitano dare?

	to know	**知っている** **shitteiru**
♡ ☐	I know, mom.	知ってるよ、ママ。 Shitteruyo mama.
♡ ☐	Hey! I know you.	あ！だれか知ってる。 A! Dareka shitteru.
♡ ☐	I know the answer!	答え、知ってる！ Kotae shitteru!

USE JAPANESE AT HOME

L

learn it!

♥ ☑ *Got it!*

	the lake	湖 **mizuumi**
♡ ☐	The lake is so beautiful.	湖、すごく綺麗だね。 Mizuumi sugoku kireidane.
♡ ☐	We're going swimming in the lake.	湖で泳ぐよ。 Mizuumide oyoguyo.
♡ ☐	**Later.**	あとで。 **Atode.**
♡ ☐	We will play later.	あとで遊ぼうね。 Atode asoboune.

USE JAPANESE AT HOME

L

We will come back later. あとでまた来ようね。
Atode mata koyoune.

You can have candy later. 飴は、あとで食べようね。
Amewa atode tabeyoune.

You can finish later. あとで仕上げようね。
Atode shiageyoune.

to laugh 笑う
warau

It was so funny. すごくおもしろかった。
Sugoku omoshirokatta.

We all started laughing. みんな笑い出しちゃった。
Minna warai dashichatta.

I can't stop laughing. 笑いが止まらない。
Waraiga tomaranai.

Don't laugh. 笑わないで。
Warawanaide.

the laundry 洗濯
sentaku

The clothes are clean. そっちの服は綺麗だよ。
Socchino fukuwa kireidayo.

152 TALKBOX.MOM

L

♥ ☑

♡ ☐ The clothes are dirty. そっちの服は汚れてるね。
Socchino fukuwa yogoreterune.

♡ ☐ Let's put the clothes in the washing machine. 洗濯機に服を入れよう。
Sentakukini fukuwo ireyou.

♡ ☐ Let's put the soap in. 洗剤を入れよう。
Senzaiwo ireyou.

♡ ☐ Let's start the washing machine. 洗濯機、回そう。
Sentakuki mawasou.

♡ ☐ Let's start the dryer. 乾燥機、回そう。
Kansouki mawasou.

♡ ☐ Let's move the clothes into the dryer. 服を乾燥機に入れよう。
Fukuwo kansoukini ireyou.

♡ ☐ Let's hang the clothes up to dry. 洗濯物、干そう。
Sentakumono hosou.

♡ ☐ Let's fold the clothes. 洗濯物、たたもう。
Sentakumono tatamou.

♡ ☐ Let's put the clothes away. 洗濯物、片付けよう。
Sentakumono katazukeyou.

> CHORE CARDS AND CHECKLISTS FOR CLEANING UP AT HOME IN THE TALKBOX.MOM SUBSCRIPTION

USE JAPANESE AT HOME

L

the leaf 葉っぱ
happa

The leaves are falling from the trees. 木から葉っぱが落ちてるね。
Kikara happaga ochiterune.

Here is a leaf. はい、葉っぱ。
Hai happa.

Pick up the leaf. 葉っぱ、拾って。
Happa hirotte.

ILLUSTRATED NATURE GUIDES + SCAVENGER HUNTS IN THE TALKBOX.MOM ACADEMY

---

to lie うそ
uso

Are you lying to me? 嘘ついてる？
Uso tsuiteru?

Tell me the truth. 本当のこと言って。
Hontouno koto itte.

Mom, I lied about something. ママ、嘘ついちゃったんだ。
Mama uso tsuichattanda.

L

to turn the lights off 電気を消す
denkiwo kesu

Turn the lights off. 電気を消して。
Denkiwo keshite.

Keep the lights off. 電気、消したままにしておいて。
Denki keshitamamani shiteoite.

It's time to turn the lights off. 電気を消す時間だよ。
Denkiwo kesu jikandayo.

Do you want me to turn the lights off? 電気消してあげようか？
Denki keshite ageyouka?

Do you want to turn the lights off? 電気消したい？
Denki keshitai?

to turn the lights on 電気をつける
denkiwo tsukeru

Turn the lights on. 電気をつけて。
Denkiwo tsukete.

Turn the lights back on. また電気、つけて。
Mata denki tsukete.

Do you want me to turn the lights on? 電気つけてあげようか？
Denki tsukete ageyouka?

Do you want to turn the lights on? 電気つけたい？
Denki tsuketai?

L

Keep the lights on. 電気、つけたままにしておいて。
Denki tsuketamamani shiteoite.

to like 好き
suki

I like to swim, play with my friends, and stay up late.
(for a female)
私は、スイミングと、友達と遊ぶことと、夜遅くまで起きていることが好きです。
Watashiwa suiminguto tomodachito asobukototo yoruosokumade okiteirukotoga sukidesu.

(for a male)
ぼくは、スイミングと、友達と遊ぶことと、夜遅くまで起きていることが好きです。
Bokuwa suiminguto tomodachito asobukototo yoruosokumade okiteirukotoga sukidesu.

I like cookies. クッキーが好き。
Kukkiiga suki.

I like your teacher. *(Name)*先生が好き。
*(Name)*senseiga suki.

I like Michael.
(like a crush)
マイケルのことが大好き。
Maikeru no kotoga daisuki.

L

to listen 話を聞く
hanashiwo kiku

Listen to me. お話聞いて。
Ohanashi kiite.

I am listening to you. ちゃんと聞いてるよ。
Chanto kiiteruyo.

You are not listening to me. お話聞いてないでしょ。
Ohanashi kiite naidesho.

Will you please listen to me? ちゃんとお話聞いてくれる？
Chanto ohanashi kiite kureru?

Look! 見て！
Mite!

Look at the dog. あの犬見て。
Ano inu mite.

Look at the tree. あの木見て。
Ano ki mite.

Look at the table. テーブル見て。
Teeburu mite.

What are you looking at? 何見てるの？
Nani miteruno?

I'm looking at a bird. 鳥見てるの。
Tori miteruno.

L

- ♥ ☑
- ♡ ☐ At nothing. I'm thinking. 別に何も。考えごとしてるだけ。
Betsuni nanimo. Kangaegoto shiteru dake.
- ♡ ☐ Look right there. そこ見て。
Soko mite.
- ♡ ☐ Look up. 上見て。
Ue mite.
- ♡ ☐ Look out the window. 窓の外見て。
Madono soto mite.
- ♡ ☐ Don't look! 見ちゃダメ!
Micha dame!

ILLUSTRATED NATURE GUIDES + SCAVENGER HUNTS IN THE TALKBOX.MOM ACADEMY

to lose なくす
nakusu

- ♡ ☐ Did you lose your blanket? 毛布無くしちゃったの?
Moufu nakushichattano?
- ♡ ☐ Did you lose your toy? おもちゃ無くしちゃったの?
Omocha nakushichattano?
- ♡ ☐ I lost my blanket. 毛布無くしちゃった。
Moufu nakushichatta.

L

Where did you leave your blanket last?
毛布、最後にどこに持って行ったか覚えてる？
Moufu, saigoni dokoni motte ittaka oboeteru?

I don't know.
わかんない。
Wakannai.

Let's go find your blanket.
毛布探しに行こう。
Moufu sagashini ikou.

I found your blanket.
毛布、あったよ。
Moufu attayo.

You found your blanket!
毛布、あったね！
Moufu attane!

I'm lost.
迷子になっちゃった。
Maigoni nacchatta.

> LABEL CARDS FOR HOW TO USE COMMON ITEMS IN THE BATHROOM IN THE TALKBOX.MOM SUBSCRIPTION

the lotion ローション
rooshon

Would you like some lotion on your hands?
手に少しローション塗る？
Teni sukoshi rooshon nuru?

I need some lotion.
ローション、塗らなきゃ。
Rooshon nuranakya.

USE JAPANESE AT HOME

L

Let's put on your lotion.
ローション、塗ろうね。
Rooshon nuroune.

Put some lotion on.
ローション、塗って。
Rooshon nutte.

Rub your lotion in a little more.
もう少し、しっかり塗り込んで。
Mousukoshi shikkari nurikonde.

loud うるさい
urusai

You are too loud.
うるさいよ。
Urusaiyo.

Use your inside voice.
お部屋の中の声の大きさでお話しして。
Oheyano nakano koeno ookisade ohanashi shite.

Please don't be so loud.
そんなにうるさくしないで。
Sonnani urusaku shinaide.

Would you please say that louder?
もっと大きな声で言って。
Motto ookina koede itte.

L

to love 大好き
daisuki

I love you. 大好きだよ。
Daisukidayo.

I love my school. 学校大好き。
Gakkou daisuki.

I love riding my bike. 自転車乗るの大好き。
Jitensha noruno daisuki.

M

learn it!

♥ ☑ *Got it!*

	the magazine	雑誌 **zasshi**
♡ ☐	I'm reading a magazine.	雑誌読んでるの。 Zasshi yonderuno.
♡ ☐	Please don't rip the pages out of my magazine.	雑誌のページ切り取らないでよ。 Zasshino peeji kiritoranaideyo.
♡ ☐	Do you want to look at this magazine with me?	一緒にこの雑誌見たい？ Isshoni kono zasshi mitai?

USE JAPANESE AT HOME

M

magic 魔法
mahou

It's magic! 魔法だよ!
Mahoudayo!

I did it with magic. 魔法かけたんだよ。
Mahou kaketandayo.

the mail 郵便
yuubin

The mail is here! 郵便きたよ!
Yuubin kitayo!

Did you get the mail? 郵便は受け取った?
Yuubinwa uketotta?

I got the mail already. 郵便もう受け取ったよ。
Yuubin mou uketottayo.

to make 作る
tsukuru

Let's make a car with the play dough. 粘土で車作ろう。
Nendode kuruma tsukurou.

Let's make a snowman with the play dough. 粘土で雪だるま作ろう。
Nendode yukidaruma tsukurou.

M

Let's make a pizza with the play dough.
粘土でピザ作ろう。
Nendode piza tsukurou.

Let's make a fort.
基地を作ろう。
Kichiwo tsukurou.

Let's make a wish.
お願いごとしよう。
Onegaigoto shiyou.

Make a wish.
お願いごとして。
Onegaigoto shite.

the medicine 薬
kusuri

It's time to take your medicine.
お薬飲む時間だよ。
Okusuri nomu jikandayo.

Did you take your medicine?
お薬もう飲んだ？
Okusuri mou nonda?

Did you remember to take your medicine?
お薬忘れずに飲んだ？
Okusuri wasurezuni nonda?

I have to take medicine before I eat.
ご飯食べる前に、薬飲まないと。
Gohan taberumaeni kusuri nomanaito.

I have to take medicine every day.
毎日薬を飲まなきゃいけないんだ。
Mainichi kusuriwo nomanakya ikenainda.

USE JAPANESE AT HOME

M

the mess 散らかしたもの
chirakashita mono

Who made this mess?
誰が散らかしたの？
Darega chirakashitano?

Come over here, and clean up your mess.
こっちに来て、自分で散らかしたものは、自分で片付けて。
Kocchini kite, jibunde chirakashita monowa jibunde katazukete.

Help your (*older*) brother clean up the mess.
お兄ちゃんが片付けるの手伝ってあげて。
Oniichanga katazukeruno tetsudatte agete.

Help your (*younger*) brother clean up the mess.
弟が片付けるの手伝ってあげて。
Otoutoga katazukeruno tetsudatte agete.

Help your (*older*) sister clean up the mess.
お姉ちゃんが片付けるの手伝ってあげて。
Oneechanga katazukeruno tetsudatte agete.

Help your (*younger*) sister clean up the mess.
妹が片付けるの手伝ってあげて。
Imoutoga katazukeruno tesudatte agete.

LANGUAGE GUIDE FOR CLEANING UP ALL KINDS OF MESSES IN THE TALKBOX.MOM SUBSCRIPTION

M

messy 汚い
kitanai

The house is so messy.
家が本当に汚い。
Iega hontouni kitanai.

Your room is messy.
部屋が汚いよ。
Heyaga kitanaiyo.

You need to clean it before you can go out to play.
遊びに行く前に、片付けて。
Asobini ikumaeni katazukete.

You need to clean it before you can go to your friend's house.
お友達の家に行く前に、片付けて。
Otomodachino ieni ikumaeni katazukete.

to be missing 無くなる
nakunaru

You're missing a sock.
靴下、片方なくなっちゃってるよ。
Kutsushita katahou nakunacchatteruyo.

One sandwich is missing.
サンドイッチが一つないよ。
Sandoicchiga hitotsu naiyo.

My child is missing.
こどもがいなくなっちゃった。
Kodomoga inaku nacchatta.

M

the moon 月
tsuki

It's a full moon. 満月だね。
Mangetsudane.

Where is the moon tonight? 今夜は、お月さまどこにいるかな？
Konyawa otsukisama dokoni irukana?

There! あそこだ！
Asokoda!

Do you see the moon? お月様みえる？
Otsukisama mieru?

ILLUSTRATED CHART FOR YOUR CLEANING CLOSET & CLEANING GUIDE IN THE TALKBOX.MOM SUBSCRIPTION

---

to mop モップをかける
moppuwo kakeru

The floor is disgusting. 床が汚い。
Yukaga kitanai.

I need to mop the floor. 床モップかけなきゃ。
Yuka moppu kakenakya.

Careful! The floor is slippery. I'm mopping it. 気をつけて！床、滑りやすいよ。今モップかけてるから。
Kiwo tsukete! Yuka suberiyasuiyo. Ima moppu kaketerukara.

M

- ♥ ☑ Please mop the floor. 床、モップかけてくれる? Yuka moppu kakete kureru?

- ♡ ☐ **More, please!** もっとください! **Motto kudasai!**
- ♡ ☐ I would like some more. もう少し欲しい 。 Mou sukoshi hoshii.
- ♡ ☐ Please give me more. もっとください。 Motto kudasai.
- ♡ ☐ Do you want some more? もっと欲しい? Motto hoshii?

- **the movie** 映画 **eiga**
- ♡ ☐ Let's watch a movie! 映画観よう! Eiga miyou!
- ♡ ☐ Which movie do you want to watch? どの映画見たい? Dono eiga mitai?
- ♡ ☐ That is not a kids movie. それは、こどもの映画じゃないよ。 Sorewa kodomono eigaja naiyo.
- ♡ ☐ Is this your favorite movie? これ、好きな映画? Kore sukina eiga?

M

the music 音楽
ongaku

Let's listen to some music.
音楽聴こうか。
Ongaku kikouka.

I'm turning on the music.
音楽かけるよ。
Ongaku kakeruyo.

Please turn off the music.
音楽消して。
Ongaku keshite.

This is my favorite song.
この歌大好きなんだ。
Kono uta daisukinanda.

Turn up the music!
音大きくして！
Oto ookiku shite!

Turn down the music.
音小さくして。
Oto chiisaku shite.

My baby loves music.
赤ちゃん、音楽大好きなんだ。
Akachan ongaku daisukinanda.

N

learn it!

♥☑ *Got it!*

the nap お昼寝
ohirune

♡☐ You need to take a nap. — お昼寝しなきゃね。 Ohirune shinakyane.

♡☐ It's nap time. — お昼寝の時間だよ。 Ohiruneno jikandayo.

♡☐ It's time for your nap. — お昼寝する時間だよ。 Ohirune suru jikandayo.

♡☐ Did you have a nice nap? — よく眠れた？ Yoku nemureta?

♡☐ He/She didn't nap long enough. — ちょっとしかお昼寝しなかった。 Chottoshika ohirune shinakatta.

USE JAPANESE AT HOME

N

- ♥ ☑ He/She napped for a very long time. — たくさんお昼寝した。 Takusan ohirune shita.
- ♡ ☐ Stay in your room during nap time. — お昼寝の時間なんだから、部屋から出て来ちゃダメ。 Ohiruneno jikan nandakara heyakara detekicha dame.
- ♡ ☐ Don't come out. — 部屋から出てこないで。 Heyakara dete konaide.

naughty やんちゃ
yancha

- ♡ ☐ You are being so naughty. — ちょっとふざけすぎだよ。 Chotto fuzakesugidayo.
- ♡ ☐ That was naughty. — お行儀悪いよ。 Ogyougi waruiyo.
- ♡ ☐ You need to shape up. — ちゃんとしなきゃダメだよ。 Chanto shinakya damedayo.

to need (something) ...がいる。 **...ga iru.**

to need (to do something) ...しなきゃ。 **...shinakaya.**

- ♡ ☐ I need to go pee. — おしっこしなきゃ。 Oshikko shinakya.

N

- [x] I need my binky. おしゃぶりがいる。
  Oshaburiga iru.
- [ ] I need you to listen. お話聞いて。
  Ohanashi kiite.
- [ ] You have to wash your hands. 手を洗わなきゃ。
  Tewo arawanakya.

- [ ] **Next time!** 今度ね!
  Kondone!
- [ ] Next time we'll go to the park. 今度は、公園行こうね。
  Kondowa kouen ikoune.

- **next to** 隣
  tonari
- [ ] Your backpack is next to the couch. リュックは、ソファーの横にあるよ。
  Ryukkuwa sofaano yokoni aruyo.
- [ ] You need to stand next to your (*older*) brother. お兄ちゃんのすぐ横に立っててね。
  Oniichanno sugu yokoni tattetene.
- [ ] You need to stand next to your (*younger*) brother. 弟のすぐ横に立っててね。
  Otoutono sugu yokoni tattetene.

USE JAPANESE AT HOME

N

	You need to stand next to your (*older*) sister.	お姉ちゃんのすぐ横に立っててね。 Oneechanno sugu yokoni tattetene.
	You need to stand next to your (*younger*) sister.	妹のすぐ横に立っててね。 Imoutono sugu yokoni tattetene.

	nice	優しい **yasashii**
	You are so nice.	優しいね。 Yasashiine.
	You are so nice to your friend.	おともだちに優しいね。 Otomodachini yasashiine.
	Be nice.	優しくね。 Yasashikune.

	No.	いいえ.。/ ダメ。 **Iie. / Dame.**
	No, thank you. (*for a child*)	ううん、いらない。 Uun, iranai.
	(*for an adult*)	結構です。 Kekkou desu.

174　TALKBOX.MOM

N

Never.	絶対ダメ。	Zettai dame.
Never again.	もう絶対ダメだからね。	Mou zettai dame dakarane.
No. Don't ask again.	ダメ、もう聞かないで。	Dame, mou kikanide.
I already said, "No."	ダメって言ったでしょ。	Damette ittadesho.
I don't like the chair.	この椅子嫌い。	Kono isu kirai.
I don't like it either. (*for a male*)	ぼくも好きじゃない。	Bokumo sukijanai.
(*for a female*)	私も好きじゃない。	Watashimo sukijanai.

the noise 騒音
souon

What is that noise?	何の音？	Nanno oto?
Are you making that noise?	大きい音たててるの (*name*)?	Ookii oto tateteruno (*name*)?
Please don't be so noisy.	そんなにうるさくしないで。	Sonnani urusaku shinaide.

USE JAPANESE AT HOME

N

Now! 今！
Ima!

Right this second. 今すぐ！
Ima sugu!

to nurse 母乳をあげる
bonyuuwo ageru

I need to nurse the baby. 赤ちゃんにミルクあげなきゃ。
Akachanni miruku agenakya.

I need to nurse the baby in two hours. あと２時間したら、赤ちゃんにミルクあげなきゃ。
Ato nijikan shitara akachanni miruku agenakya.

LANGUAGE GUIDE FOR BREASTFEEDING & BOTTLES IN THE TALKBOX.MOM SUBSCRIPTION

O

learn it!

♥ ☑ *Got it!*

the ocean **海**
umi

♡ ☐ The ocean is so big. 海、すごく大きいね。
Umi, sugoku ookiine.

♡ ☐ Look how the waves crash on the shore. 波が海岸に打ち寄せるの、見て。
Namiga kaiganni uchiyoseruno mite.

off **離れる**
hanareru

♡ ☐ Please take your shoes off. 靴をぬいでね。
Kutsuwo nuidene.

USE JAPANESE AT HOME

O

♥ ☑
♡ ☐ Please get off the table. テーブルから降りてね。
Teeburukara oritene.

♡ ☐ Turn off the lights. 電気消して。
Denki keshite.

♡ ☐ Get off of your (*older*) brother. お兄ちゃんから離れて。
Oniichankara hanarete.

♡ ☐ Get off of your (*younger*) brother. 弟から離れて。
Otoutokara hanarete.

♡ ☐ Get off of your (*older*) sister. お姉ちゃんから離れて。
Oneechankara hanarete.

♡ ☐ Get off of your (*younger*) sister. 妹から離れて。
Imoutokara hanarete.

old 古い
furui

older 年上
toshiue

♡ ☐ The food is old. (*rotten*) この食べ物は古くなってるよ。
Kono tabemonowa furuku natteruyo.

♡ ☐ That is an old toy. あれは、古いおもちゃだよ。
Arewa furui omochadayo.

♡ ☐ He/She is older. (*Name*)の方が年上。
(*Name*)no houga toshiue.

O

He is my oldest son. (Name)は長男です。
(Name)wa chounandesu.

She is my oldest daughter. (Name)は長女です。
(Name)wa choujodesu.

to get on (*something*) 乗る
noru

Do you want to go on my shoulders? 肩車してもらいたい？
Kataguruma shite moraitai?

Get on my back! おんぶするから、乗って！
Onbu surukara notte!

Get on your bike. 自転車に乗って。
Jitenshani notte.

Do you need help getting on the bike? 自転車に乗るの手伝おうか？
Jitenshani noruno tetsudaouka?

Do you want to go on the rocking horse? 木馬に乗りたい？
Mokubani noritai?

to open 開ける
akeru

Do you want me to open the bottle for you? ビン開けてあげようか？
Bin akete ageyouka?

O

- Do you want me to open the box for you? — 箱開けてあげようか？ Hako akete ageyouka?
- Open the box, please. — 箱を開けてください。 Hakowo akete kudasai.
- Open the door, please. — ドアを開けてください。 Doawo akete kudasai.
- Open the jar, please. — ビンを開けてください。 Binwo akete kudasai.
- Open the cupboard, please. — 食器棚を開けてください。 Shokkidanawo akete kudasai.
- Open the drawer, please. — 引き出しを開けてください。 Hikidashiwo akete kudasai.
- Please open this for me. *(food in a bag)* — これ開けて。 Kore akete.

to get out of から降りる **kara oriru**

to come out of から出る **kara deru**

- Do you want to get out of the stroller? — ベビーカーから降りたいの？ Bebiikaa kara oritaino?
- Do you want to come out of your crib? — ベビーベッドから出たいの？ Bebiibeddo kara detaino?

O

- ♥ ☑ Do you want to come out of your highchair? — お椅子から降りたいの？ Oisu kara oritaino?
- ♡ ☐ Do you want to come out of your car seat? — チャイルドシートから降りたいの？ Chairudoshiito kara oritaino?
- ♡ ☐ You can't come out of your car seat yet. — チャイルドシートから出てはいけませんよ。 Chairudoshiito kara detewa ikemasenyo.

outside 外
soto

- ♡ ☐ Let's play outside? — 外で遊ぼう! Sotode asobou!
- ♡ ☐ Do you want to play outside? — 外で遊びたい？ Sotode asobitai?
- ♡ ☐ He/She went outside. — 外に行ったよ。 Sotoni ittayo.

> GUIDES, CHARTS & ACTIVITIES FOR PLAYING OUTSIDE IN THE TALKBOX.MOM SUBSCRIPTION

USE JAPANESE AT HOME

P

learn it!

♥ ☑ *Got it!*

the park 公園
kouen

♥ ☐ Let's go to the park. 公園行こう。
Kouen ikou.

♥ ☐ We're at the park! 公園、着いたよ！
(when you just arrive) Kouen tsuitayo!

♥ ☐ Do you want to go 滑り台すべりたい？
down the slide? Suberidai suberitai?

♥ ☐ Do you want to go on ブランコのりたい？
the swings? Buranko noritai?

> LANGUAGE GUIDE FOR THE PARK IN THE TALKBOX.MOM SUBSCRIPTION

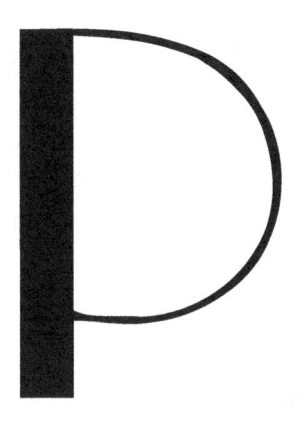

USE JAPANESE AT HOME

P

the path 道
michi

Follow the path. 道に沿っていって。
Michini sotte itte.

Stay on the path. 道からそれちゃダメだよ。
Michikara sorecha damedayo.

the pet ペット
petto

What kind of pet do you have? どんなペット飼ってるの?
Donna petto katteruno?

I have a fish. 魚飼ってるんだ。
Sakana katterunda.

I have a cat. 猫飼ってるんだ。
Neko katterunda.

I have a dog. 犬飼ってるんだ。
Inu katterunda.

I have a hamster. ハムスター飼ってるんだ。
Hamusutaa katterunda.

I have a rat. ネズミ飼ってるんだ。
Nezumi katterunda.

I have a bird. 鳥飼ってるんだ。
Tori katterunda.

P

I have a snake. へび飼ってるんだ。
Hebi katterunda.

I have a lizard. トカゲ飼ってるんだ。
Tokage katterunda.

Did you feed the dog? 犬にエサあげた？
Inuni esa ageta?

Please feed the dog. 犬にエサあげて。
Inuni esa agete.

I fed the dog already. もう犬にエサあげたよ。
Mou inuni esa agetayo.

to pet 撫でる
naderu

May we pet your dog? 犬を撫でてもいいですか？
Inuwo nadetemo iidesuka?

Please do not pet my dog. 犬を撫でないでください。
Inuwo nadenaide kudasai.

My dog isn't good with kids. うちの犬、子どもがあまり好きじゃないんです。
Uchino inu kodomoga amari sukija naindesu.

My dog is really good with kids. うちの犬、子どもが大好きなんです。
Uchino inu kodomoga daisuki nandesu.

USE JAPANESE AT HOME

p

- ♥ ☑
- ♡ ☐ Do you want to pet the dog? — 犬を撫でたい？ Inuwo nadetai?
- ♡ ☐ Pet the dog gently. — 優しく撫でてあげてね。 Yasashiku nadete agetene.
- ♡ ☐ The cat likes to be petted. — その猫は、撫でられるのが好きなんだよね。 Sono nekowa naderarerunoga suki nandayone.
- ♡ ☐ The cat hates people. — その猫は、人があまり好きじゃないの。 Sono nekowa hitoga amari sukija naino.
- ♡ ☐ Don't pet the cat. — 猫を撫でないでね。 Nekowo nadenaidene.

the phone 電話
denwa

- ♡ ☐ The phone is ringing! — 電話が鳴ってるよ！ Denwaga natteruyo!
- ♡ ☐ Pick up the phone. — 電話に出て。 Denwani dete.
- ♡ ☐ Don't pick up the phone. — 電話には出ないで。 Denwaniwa denaide.
- ♡ ☐ Hang up the phone. — 電話、切って。 Denwa kitte.

P

to pick up 片付ける
(put away) **katazukeru**

(people) 迎えに行く
mukaeni ku

Please pick up your toys.	おもちゃ片付けてね。 Omocha katazuketene.
Let's pick up your toys.	おもちゃ片付けようね。 Omocha katazukeyoune.
You have five minutes to pick up your toys.	おもちゃ、5分で片付けてね。 Omocha gofunde katazuketene.
Please help me pick up the toys.	おもちゃ片付けるの手伝って。 Omocha katazukeruno tetsudatte.
Pick up your (item).	(Item) 片付けて。 (Item) katazukete.
Please pick me up after school.	学校が終わったら迎えに来てね。 Gakkou ga owattara, mukaeni kitene.

the pillow 枕
makura

Do not give the baby a pillow.	枕、赤ちゃんにはあげないで。 Makura akachanniwa agenaide.
You drooled on my pillow. (for a female)	私の枕によだれ垂らしたでしょ。 Watashino makurani yodare tarashitadesho.

USE JAPANESE AT HOME   187

P

(for a male) ぼくの枕によだれ垂らしたでしょ。
Bokuno makurani yodare tarashitadesho.

Put the pillows in a pile, and we'll jump on them. 枕を重ねて、上でジャンプしよう。
Makurawo kasanete, uede janpu shiyou.

the plant 植物
shokubutsu

Did you water the plants? 植物にお水あげた？
Shokubutsuni omizu ageta?

Please. お願いします．
Onegaishimasu.

Say, "Please." 「お願いします」って言って。
"Onegaishimasu"tte itte.

to plug something in コンセントに入れる
konsentoni ireru

Would you please plug in my cell phone? ケータイ充電してくれる？
Keetai juuden shitekureru?

P

♥☑			
♡☐		Please plug in my phone. (cell phone)	ケータイ充電して。 Keetai juuden shite.
♡☐		Would you please plug in my tablet?	タブレット充電してくれる？ Taburetto juuden shitekureru?
♡☐		Please unplug my tablet.	タブレットのコンセント抜いて。 Taburettono konsento nuite.
♡☐		Please don't plug in my tablet.	タブレットのコンセント入れないで。 Taburettono konsento irenaide.
♡☐		Please don't unplug my phone.	ケータイのコンセント抜かないで。 Keetaino konsento nukanaide.
♡☐		Don't touch the outlet. It's dangerous.	コンセントに触っちゃダメだよ。危ないからね。 Konsentoni sawaccha damedayo. Abunaikarane.
		the poop	うんち **unchi**
♡☐		Look out! Don't step in the poop.	気をつけて！うんち踏んじゃダメだよ。 Kiwo tsukete! Unchi funja damedayo.
♡☐		Your stomach hurts?	お腹痛い？ Onaka itai?

USE JAPANESE AT HOME

P

♥ ☑

♡ ☐ Did you poop today? 今日、うんちでた？
Kyou unchi deta?

♡ ☐ Sit on the toilet, and try to poop. トイレに座って、頑張ってうんちしてみよう。
Toireni suwatte ganbatte unchi shitemiyou.

♡ ☐ I need to poop. うんちしたい。
Unchi shitai.

♡ ☐ The baby pooped in his/her diaper. 赤ちゃんが、オムツでうんちした。
Akachanga omutsude unchi shita.

♡ ☐ The baby pooped up his/her back. 赤ちゃん、うんちが漏れて、背中までいっちゃった。
Akachan unchiga morete senakamade icchatta.

STEP BY STEP GUIDES FOR HELPING LITTLE ONES WITH THE POTTY IN THE TALKBOX.MOM SUBSCRIPTION

---

the potty トイレ
toire

♡ ☐ I need to use the potty. おトイレ行きたい。
Otoire ikitai.

♡ ☐ Do you need to go potty? おトイレ行きたい？
Otoire ikitai?

P

♥☑			
♡☐	I need to poop.	うんちしたい。	Unchi shitai.
♡☐	I need to pee.	おしっこしたい。	Oshikko shitai.

	a little praise	**ちょっとした褒め言葉**	**chottoshita homekotoba**
♡☐	You're so smart.	頭いいね。	Atama iine.
♡☐	You're such a good girl/boy.	いい子だね。	Iiko dane.
♡☐	You're so strong!	強いね!	Tsuyoine!
♡☐	You're so fast!	速いね!	Hayaine!
♡☐	You're so cute!	可愛いね!	Kawaiine!
♡☐	You're so handsome!	かっこいいね!	Kakkoiine!
♡☐	You're so beautiful.	きれいね。	Kireine.
♡☐	You're so good at school.	お勉強が得意なんだね。	Obenkyouga tokui nandane.

USE JAPANESE AT HOME

P

You're so good at sports. 運動が得意なんだね。
Undouga tokui nandane.

You always do such a good job. いつも上手にできるね。
Itsumo jouzuni dekirune.

the present プレゼント
purezento

I/We got you a present. プレゼントがあるんだ。
Purezentoga arunda.

You can open your presents. プレゼント、開けていいよ。
Purezento akete iiyo.

I'm opening my present! プレゼント、開けるよ！
Purezento akeruyo!

the puddle 水たまり
mizutamari

Don't walk in the puddle. 水たまりの中を歩かないで。
Mizutamarino nakawo arukanaide.

Let's jump in the puddles. 水たまりの中でジャンプしちゃおう。
Mizutamarino nakade janpu shichaou.

P

to pull 引く
hiku

Pull the door. ドア、引いて。
Doa hiite.

Don't pull on my shirt. シャツ引っ張らないで。
Shatsu hipparanaide.

to push 押す
osu

Don't push. 押さないで。
Osanaide.

Did you push your (*older*) brother? お兄ちゃんのこと押した？
Oniichanno koto oshita?

Did you push your (*younger*) brother? 弟のこと押した？
Otoutono koto oshita?

Did you push your (*older*) sister? お姉ちゃんのこと押した？
Oneechanno koto oshita?

Did you push your (*younger*) sister? 妹のこと押した？
Imoutono koto oshita?

Push the door. ドア、押して。
Doa oshite.

Q

learn it!

♥ ☑ *Got it!*

♡ ☐   **Quick!**   早く!
                                Hayaku!

♡ ☐   **Quiet.**   静かに。
                                Shizukani.

♡ ☐   Please be quiet.   静かにしてね。
                                Shizukani shitene.

♡ ☐   Please be quieter.   もうちょっと静かにしてね。
                                Mou chotto shizukani shitene.

USE JAPANESE AT HOME

Q

♥☑ ♡☐	Why is he/she being so quiet?	(Name)は、なんでそんなに静かにしてるの? (Name)wa, nande sonnani shizukani shiteruno?
♡☐	It's really quiet.	本当に静かだね。 Hontouni shizukadane.
♡☐	If the kids are quiet, we know they are getting into trouble.	子どもたちが静かな時は、たいてい悪いことしてる時なんだよね。 Kodomotachiga shizukana tokiwa taitei waruikoto shiteru toki nandayone.

R

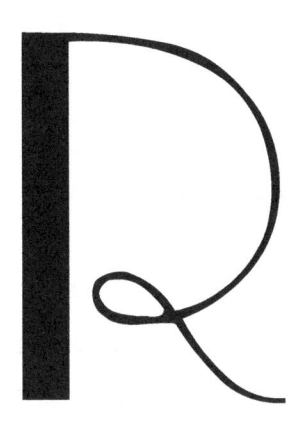

learn it!

♥ ☑ *Got it!*

	the rainbow	虹
		niji
♡ ☐	Look at that beautiful rainbow.	あの綺麗な虹見て。 Ano kireina niji mite.
♡ ☐	After it rains, there is a rainbow.	雨が上がれば、虹が出てくる。 Amega agareba nijiga detekuru.
	the rattle	ガラガラ
		garagara
♡ ☐	Here is your rattle.	はい、ガラガラだよ。 Hai, garagaradayo.

USE JAPANESE AT HOME

R

♥ ☑
♡ ☐ Shake your rattle. ガラガラ、振ってみて。
Garagara futtemite.

to read 読む
yomu

♡ ☐ Would you like to read together? 一緒に読もうか？
Isshoni yomouka?

♡ ☐ Let's read together. 一緒に読もうね。
Isshoni yomoune.

♡ ☐ I love reading with you. 一緒に本読むの大好き。
Isshoni hon yomuno daisuki.

♡ ☐ We read together every day. 毎日一緒に本を読んでるんだ。
Mainichi isshoni honwo yonderunda.

> GET THE GOING OUT THE DOOR GUIDE IN THE TALKBOX.MOM SUBSCRIPTION

♡ ☐ **Ready!** 準備できた！
Junbi dekita!

♡ ☐ Please get ready to go. 行く準備してください。
Iku jjunbi shite kudasai.

R

- [x] Are you ready? 準備できた?
Junbi dekita?
- [ ] Is everyone ready to go? みんな、行く準備できた?
Minna iku junbi dekita?

the river 川
kawa

- [ ] The river is going very fast. 川の流れが速くなってきてるよ。
Kawano nagarega hayaku natte kiteruyo.
- [ ] The river is going very slow. 川の流れがゆっくりになってきてるよ。
Kawano nagarega yukkurini natte kiteruyo.
- [ ] Don't go in the river. 川に入っちゃダメ。
Kawani haiccha dame.

the rock 石
ishi

the pebble 小石
koishi

- [ ] What a cool rock! わあ、かっこいい石!
Waa kakkoii ishi!

R

- ♥ ☑
- ♡ ☐ Don't throw rocks. 石を投げちゃダメ。
  Ishiwo nagecha dame.
- ♡ ☐ I want to take this rock home. この石、お家に持って帰りたい。
  Kono ishi ouchini motte kaeritai.

to roll 転がる
korogaru

- ♡ ☐ The baby can roll over. 赤ちゃん、寝返りできるよ。
  Akachan negaeri dekiruyo.
- ♡ ☐ Let's roll down the hill. 坂を転がって降りよう。
  Sakawo korogatte oriyou.
- ♡ ☐ Roll the ball. ボール、転がして。
  Booru korogashite.
- ♡ ☐ Roll the ball to me. *(for a male)* ボール、ぼくに転がして。
  Booru bokuni korogashite.
- ♡ ☐ *(for a female)* ボール、私に転がして。
  Booru watashini korogashite.

FUN ACTIVITY FOR ACTIONS, LIKE ROLL + DUCK, IN THE TALKBOX.MOM SUBSCRIPTION

S

learn it!

♥ ☑ *Got it!*

	same	同じ
		onaji
♡ ☐	He/She got more than I did.	(Name)の方が多い。 (Name)no houga ooi.
♡ ☐	You got the same.	同じだよ。 Onajidayo.
♡ ☐	You're wearing the same shirt.	同じシャツ着てるね。 Onaji shatsu kiterune.
♡ ☐	Same here. (*likewise.*)	こちらこそ。 Kochirakoso.

USE JAPANESE AT HOME

S

the sand 砂
suna

He/She loves to play in the sand. (Name)は砂場で遊ぶのが大好きです。
(Name)wa sunabade asobunoga daisuki desu.

There is sand in my shoe. 靴に砂が入った。
Kutsuni sunaga haitta.

LANGUAGE GUIDES FOR THE PLAYGROUND IN THE TALKBOX.MOM SUBSCRIPTION

---

the school 学校
gakkou

What did you do at school today? 今日は学校で何やったの？
Kyouwa gakkoude nani yattano?

I played outside. 外で遊んだよ。
Sotode asondayo.

I took a test. テストを受けたよ。
Tesutowo uketayo.

I drew a picture. 絵を描いたよ。
Ewo kaitayo.

I had science today. 今日は理科があったよ。
Kyouwa rikaga attayo.

S

- I had art today. 今日は図工があったよ。
Kyouwa zukouga attayo.

- I had math today. 今日は算数があったよ。
Kyouwa sansuuga attayo.

- I had history today. 今日は歴史があったよ。
Kyouwa rekishiga attayo.

- I had music class today. 今日は音楽があったよ。
Kyouwa ongakuga attayo.

- I got in trouble. ちょっと怒られちゃった。
Chotto okorarechatta.

- What did you do? 何したの？
Nani shitano?

- I didn't listen to the teacher. *(not following instructions)* 先生の言う事きかなかったんだ。
Senseino iu koto kikanakattanda.

- *(when the teacher was speaking)* 先生の話聞いてなかったんだ。
Senseino hanashi kiite nakattanda.

- I didn't get in trouble today. 今日は悪いことしなかったよ。
Kyouwa waruikoto shinakattayo.

the scissors ハサミ
hasami

- Do you want to cut the paper? その紙、切りたい？
Sono kami kiritai?

S

♥ ☑

♡ ☐	Please cut out a heart for me.	ハートの形に切ってね。 Haatono katachini kittene.
♡ ☐	Good job cutting out a heart.	ハート、上手に切れたね。 Haato jouzuni kiretane.
♡ ☐	Can you cut a circle?	丸い形に切れる？ Marui katachini kireru?
♡ ☐	Good job cutting out a circle.	丸い形、上手に切れたね。 Marui katachi jouzuni kiretane.
♡ ☐	Cut a square.	四角く切って。 Shikakuku kitte.
♡ ☐	Good job cutting out a square.	四角、上手に切れたね。 Shikaku jouzuni kiretane.
♡ ☐	How do you walk with scissors?	ハサミを持って歩くときはどうするの？ Hasamiwo motte arukutokiwa dousuruno?
♡ ☐	Like this.	こうするの。 Kousuruno.

LANGUAGE GUIDES, WALL CHARTS, & ACTIVITIES FOR ARTS AND CRAFTS IN THE TALKBOX.MOM SUBSCRIPTION

S

♥ ☑	**the seatbelt**	シートベルト **shiitoberuto**
♡ ☐	You need to wear your seatbelt.	シートベルトしないとね。 Shiitoberuto shinaitone.
♡ ☐	Please put on your seatbelt.	シートベルトしてね。 Shiitoberuto shitene.
♡ ☐	You can't take off your seatbelt.	シートベルト、取っちゃダメ。 Shiitoberuto tocchadame.
♡ ☐	I have my seatbelt on too. *(for a female)*	私もシートベルトしてるよ。 Watashimo shiitoberuto shiteruyo.
♡ ☐	*(for a male)*	ぼくもシートベルトしてるよ。 Bokumo shiitoberuto shiteruyo.
♡ ☐	Is everyone buckled?	みんなシートベルトした？ Minna shiitoberuto shita?
♡ ☐	Buckle up!	シートベルトして！ Shiitoberuto shite!

	to see	見る **miru**
♡ ☐	Do you see the dog?	犬、見える？ Inu mieru?
♡ ☐	Do you see the bug?	虫、見える？ Mushi mieru?

S

Do you see the toy?
おもちゃ、見える?
Omocha mieru?

Stay where I can see you.
見えないところには、行かないで。
Mienai tokoroniwa ikanaide.

If you can't see me, I can't see you.
そっちから見えないってことは、こっちからも見えないんだよ。
Socchikara mienaitte kotowa kocchikaramo mienaindayo.

Do you want to see what s/he has?
(Name)が何持ってるのか、見たい?
(Name)ga nani motterunoka mitai?

the shade 日陰
hikage

Let's go in the shade.
日陰に行こう。
Hikageni ikou.

Let's sit in the shade.
日陰に座ろう。
Hikageni suwarou.

Stand in the shade.
日陰に立ってて。
Hikageni tattete.

S

❤️ ☑

	to share	**一緒に使う** **isshoni tsukau**
♡ ☐	... is not sharing with me.	......が一緒に使わせてくれない。 ...ga isshoni tsukawasete kurenai.
♡ ☐	Please share the toy.	おもちゃ、一緒に使ってね。 Omocha, isshoni tsukattene.
♡ ☐	You need to share the toy.	おもちゃ、一緒に使わないと。 Omocha, isshoni tsukawanaito.
♡ ☐	The baby doesn't know how to share.	赤ちゃんはどうやって一緒に使うかわからないんだよ。 Akachanwa douyatte isshoni tsukauka wakaranaindayo.
♡ ☐	That was so nice of you to share!	一緒に使わせてあげられて偉いね！ Isshoni tsukawasete agerarete eraine!
♡ ☐	Please share with him/her.	(Name)と一緒に使ってね。 (Name)to isshoni tsukattene.
♡ ☐	Please share with your (older) brother.	お兄ちゃんと一緒に使ってね。 Oniichanto isshoni tsukattene.
♡ ☐	Please share with your (younger) brother.	弟と一緒に使ってね。 Otoutoto isshoni tsukattene.
♡ ☐	Please share with your (older) sister.	お姉ちゃんと一緒に使ってね。 Oneechanto isshoni tsukattene.
♡ ☐	Please share with your (younger) sister.	妹と一緒に使ってね。 Imoutoto isshoni tsukattene.

S

- He/She doesn't want to share. — (Name)が一緒に使わせてくれない。 (Name)ga isshoni tsukawasete kurenai.
- Will you share some crackers with me? — クラッカーちょっとくれる？ Kurakkaa chotto kureru?
- I will share my crackers with you. — クラッカー分けてあげるよ。 Kurakkaa wakete ageruyo.
- Please share the crackers. — クラッカー分けて。 Kurakkaa wakete.

sharp 尖ってる **togatteru**

- Careful! The table is really sharp. — 気をつけて！そのテーブル、すごく尖ってるからね。 Kiwo tsukete! Sono teeburu sugoku togatteru karane.
- That knife is very sharp. — あのナイフは、すごく鋭い。 Ano naifuwa sugoku surudoi.
- Do not touch it. — 触っちゃダメだよ。 Sawaccha damedayo.
- That stick is too sharp to play with. — この棒は尖ってて危ないから、これで遊んじゃダメ。 Kono bouwa togattete abunaikara korede asonja dame.

S

the shoes 靴
kutsu

♡☐	Put your shoes away.	靴、片付けて。 Kutsu katazukete.	
♡☐	Put your shoes on.	靴、履いて。 Kutsu haite.	
♡☐	Your shoes are untied.	靴の紐ほどけてるよ。 Kutsuno himo hodoketeruyo.	
♡☐	Tie your shoes.	靴の紐結んで。 Kutsuno himo musunde.	

> LANGUAGE GUIDE FOR PUTTING ON DIFFERENT SHOES IN THE TALKBOX.MOM SUBSCRIPTION

the shovel シャベル
shaberu

♡☐	Use your shovel to dig in the sand.	シャベルを使って砂を掘ったら。 Shaberuwo tsukatte sunawo hottara.
♡☐	Fill up your bucket using the shovel.	シャベル使ってバケツいっぱいにしたら。 Shaberu tukatte baketsu ippaini shitara.

> LANGUAGE GUIDE FOR HAVING A BLAST AT THE PARK IN THE TALKBOX.MOM SUBSCRIPTION

USE JAPANESE AT HOME

S

to show 見せる
miseru

Show me what's in your mouth. 口の中に何が入っているのか見せて。
Kuchino nakani naniga haitteirunoka misete.

Show me what's in your hands. 手に何を持っているのか見せて。
Teni naniwo motteirunoka misete.

Show me. 見せて。
Misete.

Do you want me to show you how to tie your shoes? 靴紐の結び方、教えてあげようか？
Kutsuhimono musubikata oshiete ageyouka?

I'm going to show you how to... …のやり方教えてあげるね。
…no yarikata oshiete agerune.

I'm going to show you how to kick the ball. ボールの蹴り方教えてあげるね。
Booruno kerikata oshiete agerune.

sick 具合が悪い
guaiga warui

Are you sick? 具合が悪いの？
Guaiga waruino?

I'm sick. 具合が悪いの。
Guaiga waruino.

S

- ♥ ☑ He/She is sick. (Name)は具合が悪いの。
  (Name)wa guaiga waruino.
- ♡ ☐ They are all sick. みんな具合が悪いの。
  Minna guaiga waruino.
- ♡ ☐ My family is sick. 家族全員、具合が悪いの。
  Kazoku zenin guaiga waruino.
- ♡ ☐ We've been sick for a week. 一週間ずっと具合が悪いの。
  Isshuukan zutto guaiga waruino.
- ♡ ☐ I was sick yesterday. 昨日は体調が悪かったんだ。
  Kinouwa taichouga warukattanda.
- ♡ ☐ I'm getting sick. 体調が悪くなってきた。
  Taichouga waruku nattekita.
- ♡ ☐ I think I am getting sick. なんだか体調が悪くなってきたみたい。
  Nandaka taichouga waruku nattekita mitai.
- ♡ ☐ You can't play because you are sick. 具合が悪いんだから、遊べないよ。
  Guaiga waruindakara, asobenaiyo.
- ♡ ☐ You can't go to school because you are sick. 具合が悪いんだから、学校には行けないよ。
  Guaiga waruindakara, gakkouniwa ikenaiyo.
- ♡ ☐ Do you have a stomachache? お腹痛いの？
  Onaka itaino?

USE JAPANESE AT HOME

S

♥ ☑			
♡ ☐	I have a stomachache.	お腹が痛い。 Onakaga itai.	
♡ ☐	Do you have a headache?	頭痛いの？ Atama itaino?	
♡ ☐	I have a headache.	頭が痛い。 Atamaga itai.	
♡ ☐	Do you have a sore throat?	喉痛いの？ Nodo itaino?	
♡ ☐	I have a sore throat.	喉が痛い。 Nodoga itai.	
♡ ☐	Do you have a cough?	咳が出るの？ Sekiga deruno?	
♡ ☐	I have a cough.	咳が出る。 Sekiga deru.	
♡ ☐	Do you have a cold?	風邪ひいてるの？ Kaze hiiteruno?	
♡ ☐	I have a cold.	風邪ひいてるの。 Kaze hiiteruno.	
♡ ☐	Do you have the flu?	インフルエンザになっちゃったの？ Infuruenzani nacchattano?	
♡ ☐	I have the flu.	インフルエンザになっちゃった。 Infuruenzani nacchatta.	
♡ ☐	Did you throw up?	吐いたの？ Haitano?	
♡ ☐	I threw up.	吐いた。 Haita.	

S

♥ ☑		
♡ ☐	He/She threw up.	(Name)が吐いた。 (Name)ga haita.
♡ ☐	Do you have diarrhea?	下痢してるの？ Gerishiteruno?
♡ ☐	I have diarrhea.	下痢してる。 Gerishiteru.
♡ ☐	Do you have heartburn?	胸ムカムカするの？ Mune mukamukasuruno?
♡ ☐	I have heartburn.	胸がムカムカする。 Munega mukamukasuru.
♡ ☐	Do you have an earache?	耳痛い？ Mimi itai?
♡ ☐	I have an earache.	耳が痛い。 Mimiga itai.
♡ ☐	Do you have an ear infection?	中耳炎になっちゃったの？ Chuujienni nacchattano?
♡ ☐	I have an ear infection.	中耳炎になっちゃった。 Chuujienni nacchatta.
♡ ☐	Do you have pink eye?	結膜炎になっちゃったの？ Ketsumakuenni nacchattano?
♡ ☐	I have pink eye.	結膜炎になっちゃった。 Ketsumakuenni nacchatta.
♡ ☐	Do you have lice?	シラミがいるの？ Shiramiga iruno?
♡ ☐	I have lice.	シラミがいるの。 Shiramiga iruno.

USE JAPANESE AT HOME

S

♥☑		
♡☐	Not anymore. (They're gone)	もういない。 Mou inai.
♡☐	I don't have any left.	もう全部いなくなった。 Mou zenbu inakunatta.
♡☐	I'm all better.	すっかり元気になったよ。 Sukkari genkini nattayo.
♡☐	I feel a lot better.	随分良くなった。 Zuibun yokunatta.
♡☐	I feel better.	だいぶ元気になった。 Daibu genkini natta.
♡☐	I'm a lot better.	随分良くなった。 Zuibun yokunatta.
♡☐	He/She is all better.	(Name)は、すっかり元気になったよ。 (Name)wa sukkari genkini nattayo.
♡☐	He/She is a lot better.	(Name)は、随分良くなったよ。 (Name)wa zuibun yoku nattayo.

to sing 歌う
utau

♡☐	Do you want me to sing you a song?	お歌歌って欲しい？ Outa utatte hoshii?
♡☐	I love when you sing.	お歌歌ってもらうの大好きなんだ。 Outa utatte morauno daisukinanda.

S

- ♥☑ / ♡☐ You are a great singer. お歌うまいね。 Outa umaine.
- ♡☐ What are you singing? 何の歌歌ってるの？ Nanno uta utatteruno?

> LEARN TO SING SONGS IN JAPANESE IN THE TALKBOX.MOM SUBSCRIPTION

the sink 洗面台 **senmendai**

(in the bathroom) 洗面所のシンク **senmenjono shinku**

(in the kitchen) 台所のシンク **daidokorono shinku**

- ♡☐ Please wash your hands in the sink. 洗面所で手を洗ってきて。 Senmenjode tewo arattekite.
- ♡☐ Please wash your hands in the kitchen sink. 台所のシンクで手を洗ってきて。 Daidokorono shinkude tewo arattekite.
- ♡☐ Put your plate in the sink. お皿をシンクに入れて。 Osarawo shinkuni irete.

S

to sit 座る
suwaru

Please sit down. 座ってください。
Suwatte kudasai.

Do not sit down here. ここに座っちゃダメ。
Kokoni suwaccha dame.

Do not sit there. そこに座らないの。
Sokoni suwaranaino.

Sit next to me. 隣に座って。
Tonarini suwatte.

Sit next to your (*older*) brother. お兄ちゃんの隣に座って。
Oniichanno tonarini suwatte.

Sit next to your (*younger*) brother. 弟の隣に座って。
Otoutono tonarini suwatte.

Sit next to your (*older*) sister. お姉ちゃんの隣に座って。
Oneechanno tonarini suwatte.

Sit next to your (*younger*) sister. 妹の隣に座って。
Imoutono tonarini suwatte.

Do you want to sit down? 座りたい？
Suwaritai?

I need to sit down. 座らないと。
Suwaranaito.

Let's sit down for a little bit. ちょっと座って休もう。
Chotto suwatte yasumou.

S

	Sit on my lap.	お膝に座って。 Ohizani suwatte.
	I want to sit on your lap.	お膝に座りたい。 Ohizani suwaritai.
	Sit on your bottom.	お尻をついて座って。 Oshiriwo tsuite suwatte.

the sky 空
sora

	The sky is blue.	お空が青いね。 Osoraga aoine.
	There aren't any clouds in the sky.	雲ひとつない快晴だね。 Kumo hitotsu nai kaiseidane.

the sled そり
sori

	Let's go sledding!	そり滑りに行こう！ Sorisuberini ikou!
	Get on the sled.	そりに乗って。 Sorini notte.

S

to sleep 寝る
neru

It's already time to go to sleep. — もう寝る時間だよ。 Mou neru jikandayo.

The baby is sleeping. — 赤ちゃんは寝てるよ。 Akachanwa neteruyo.

Is the baby asleep or awake? — 赤ちゃん、寝てる？起きてる？ Akachan neteru? Okiteru?

He/She is asleep. — (Name)は寝ているよ。 (Name)wa neteiruyo.

He/She is awake. — (Name)は起きてるよ。 (Name)wa okiteruyo.

the slide 滑り台
suberidai

Do you want to go down the slide? — 滑り台すべりたい？ Suberidai suberitai?

Go down the slide! — 滑り台滑って！ Suberidai subette!

I'll catch you. — 捕まえちゃうよ。 Tsukamaechauyo.

Let's go down the slide. — 滑り台滑ろう。 Suberidai suberou.

S

	Ready? Go!	準備OK? よーい、どん！ Junbi OK? Yooi don!
	Slide on down!	滑って！ Subette!

to smell	匂いがする **nioiga suru**
What's that smell?	この匂い何？ Kono nioi nani?
It smells like coconut.	ココナッツみたいな匂いがする。 Kokonattsu mitaina nioiga suru.
It smells like the dog.	犬みたいな匂いがする。 Inu mitaina nioiga suru.
It smells like poop.	ウンチみたいな匂いがする。 Unchi mitaina nioiga suru.
It smells like something is burning.	何かが焦げてるみたいな匂いがする。 Nanikaga kogeteru mitaina nioiga suru.
It smells good.	いい匂いがする。 Ii nioiga suru.
It smells bad.	臭い。 Kusai.
You smell bad.	(Name) 臭いよ。 (Name) kusaiyo.

USE JAPANESE AT HOME

S

Smile! 笑って!
Waratte!

snack おやつ
oyatsu

Are you ready for your snack? そろそろおやつ食べようか?
Sorosoro oyatsu tabeyouka?

Let's eat a snack. おやつを食べよう。
Oyatsuwo tabeyou.

COMPLETE LANGUAGE GUIDES FOR EATING & DRINKING IN THE TALKBOX.MOM SUBSCRIPTION

---

to sneeze くしゃみ
kushami

I'm going to sneeze. くしゃみが出そう。
Kushamiga desou.

I keep sneezing. くしゃみが止まらない。
Kushamiga tomaranai.

Why are you sneezing so much? なんでそんなにくしゃみしてるの?
Nande sonnani kushami shiteruno?

Excuse me. 失礼。
Shitsurei.

S

♥ ☑ **to snuggle** 寄り添う
yorisou

♡ ☐ Do you want to snuggle? くっついていたいの？
Kuttsuite itaino?

♡ ☐ I want to snuggle. くっついていたいの。
Kuttsuite itaino.

♡ ☐ Let's snuggle. ペタってしてよう。
Petatte shiteyou.

♡ ☐ You are so snuggly. くっつき虫だね。
Kuttsuki mushidane.

the soap 石鹸
sekken

♡ ☐ Wash your hands with soap. 石鹸で手を洗って。
Sekkende tewo aratte.

> STEP BY STEP GUIDE FOR WASHING HANDS & A CHART FOR BATHING IN THE TALKBOX.MOM SUBSCRIPTION

♡ ☐ **Sorry!** ごめんね！
Gomenne!

♡ ☐ Tell me, "Sorry." 「ごめんなさい」は？
"Gomennasai" wa?"

USE JAPANESE AT HOME

S

	Tell him/her, "Sorry."	(Name)に「ごめんね」って言って。 (Name)ni "gomenne" tte itte.
	I'm not sorry.	悪くないもん。 Waruku naimon.
	I don't want to tell him/her sorry.	(Name)にごめんねって言いたくない。 (Name)ni gomennette iitakunai.

to spill こぼす
kobosu

	I spilled my water.	お水こぼしちゃった。 Omizu koboshichatta.
	Careful, or you will spill your juice.	気をつけて、ジュースこぼしちゃうよ。 Kiwo tsukete juusu koboshichauyo.

to spit up 吐く
haku

	The baby spit up.	赤ちゃんが吐いたよ。 Akachanga haitayo.
	The baby spit up on the couch.	赤ちゃんがソファーに吐いたよ。 Akachanga sofaani haitayo.
	The baby spit up on my shirt. *(for a female)*	赤ちゃん、私のシャツに吐いたよ。 Akachan watashino shatsuni haitayo.

S

- ❤️ ☑ (for a male) 赤ちゃん、僕のシャツに吐いたよ。
  Akachan bokuno shatsuni haitayo.
- ♡ ☐ The baby spit up on the ground. 赤ちゃんが床に吐いたよ。
  Akachanga yukani haitayo.

sports スポーツ
supootsu

- ♡ ☐ Let's play soccer. サッカーやろう。
  Sakkaa yarou.
- ♡ ☐ Let's play basketball. バスケやろう。
  Basuke yarou.
- ♡ ☐ Let's play baseball. 野球やろう。
  Yakyuu yarou.
- ♡ ☐ Let's play hockey. ホッケーやろう。
  Hokee yarou.
- ♡ ☐ Let's go swimming 泳ぎに行こう。
  Oyogini ikou.
- ♡ ☐ Let's go running. 走りに行こう。
  Hashirini ikou.
- ♡ ☐ Time for soccer practice. サッカーの練習の時間だよ。
  Sakkaano renshuuno jikandayo.

S

the star 星
hoshi

Look at the stars. あの星みて。
Ano hoshi mite.

Here's a star sticker. はい、星のシール。
Hai hoshino shiiru.

the stick 棒
bou

What a cool stick! わあ！かっこいい棒！
Waa! Kakkoii bou!

You must leave your stick outside. 棒は、お外に置いておいて。
Bouwa osotoni oite oite.

No sticks in the house. 家の中で棒はなしだよ。
Ieno nakade bouwa nashidayo.

sticker シール
shiiru

Here's a sticker. はい、シール。
Hai, shiiru.

I got a sticker at school today! 今日学校でシールもらったんだ！
Kyou gakkoude shiiru morattanda!

S

still まだ
mada

Are you still eating? まだ食べてるの?
Mada tabeteruno?

Are you still reading your book? まだ本読んでるの?
Mada hon yonderuno?

stop やめて
yamete

Stop spitting. ツバ吐くのやめて。
Tsuba hakuno yamete.

Stop hitting. 叩くのやめて。
Tatakuno yamete.

Stop fighting. ケンカやめて。
Kenka yamete.

Stop screaming. 叫ぶのやめて。
Sakebuno yamete.

Stop yelling. 大きな声出すのやめて。
Ookina koe dasuno yamete.

Stop bothering your (*older*) brother. お兄ちゃんの邪魔するのやめて。
Oniichanno jamasuruno yamete.

Stop bothering your (*younger*) brother. 弟の邪魔するのやめて。
Otoutono jamasuruno yamete.

S

♥☑		
♡☐	Stop bothering your (older) sister.	お姉ちゃんの邪魔するのやめて。 Oneechanno jamasuruno yamete.
♡☐	Stop bothering your (younger) sister.	妹の邪魔するのやめて。 Imoutono jamasuruno yamete.
♡☐	Stop teasing your (older) brother.	お兄ちゃんからかうのやめて。 Oniichan karakauno yamete.
♡☐	Stop teasing your (younger) brother.	弟からかうのやめて。 Otouto karakauno yamete.
♡☐	Stop teasing your (older) sister.	お姉ちゃんからかうのやめて。 Oneechan karakauno yamete.
♡☐	Stop teasing your (younger) sister.	妹からかうのやめて。 Imouto karakauno yamete.
♡☐	Leave him/her alone.	(Name) ほっといてあげて。 (Name) hottoite agete.
♡☐	Stop jumping on the couch.	ソファーでジャンプするのやめて。 Sofaade janpu suruno yamete.

the street 道路
douro

♡☐	We need to cross the street.	道路を渡らないと。 Dourowo wataranaito.
♡☐	Don't walk in the street.	道路を歩いちゃダメ。 Dourowo aruicha dame.

S

♥ ☑
♡ ☐ Don't play in the street. 道路で遊んじゃダメ。
Dourode asonja dame.

> LANGUAGE GUIDE FOR NEIGHBORHOOD WALKS IN THE TALKBOX.MOM ACADEMY

the stroller ベビーカー
bebiikaa

♡ ☐ Is the stroller in the car? ベビーカー、車に積んである？
Bebiikaa kurumani tsundearu?

♡ ☐ Do you want to go in the stroller? ベビーカーに乗りたい？
Bebiikaani noritai?

the sun 太陽
taiyou

♡ ☐ The sun is really strong. 日差しがすごく強いね。
Hizashiga sugoku tsuyoine.

the sunblock 日焼け止め
hiyakedome

♡ ☐ We need to put on sunblock. 日焼け止めを塗らないと。
Hiyakedomewo nuranaito.

USE JAPANESE AT HOME 227

S

♥ ☑ **the sunlight** 太陽の光
taiyouno hikari

♡ ☐ The sunlight is coming through the window. 窓から太陽の光が入ってくる。
Madokara taiyouno hikariga haittekuru.

♡ ☐ Open the curtains to let the sunlight in. カーテンを開けて、太陽の光を取り入れよう。
Kaatenwo akete taiyouno hikariwo toriireyou.

to swim 泳ぐ
oyogu

♡ ☐ Let's go swimming! 泳ぎに行こう!
Oyogini ikou!

♡ ☐ Do you know how to swim? 泳げる?
Oyogeru?

♡ ☐ I know how to swim. 泳げるよ。
Oyogeruyo.

♡ ☐ I don't know how to swim. 泳げないよ。
Oyogenaiyo.

TALKBOX.MOM

S

♥☑		**the swing**	ブランコ **buranko**
♡☐		the baby swing	赤ちゃん用ブランコ Akachanyou buranko
♡☐		The baby is in the baby swing.	赤ちゃんは、赤ちゃん用のブランコに乗ってるよ。 Akachanwa akachanyouno burankoni notteruyo.
♡☐		Do you want to swing?	ブランコしたい？ Buranko shitai?
♡☐		I want to go on the swing.	ブランコに乗りたい。 Burankoni noritai.
♡☐		Would you push me on the swing please?	ブランコ押して。 Buranko oshite.
♡☐		Higher!	もっと高く！ Motto takaku!
♡☐		Get me down from the swing.	ブランコから降ろして。 Buranko kara oroshite.

> LANGUAGE GUIDE FOR HAVING A BLAST AT THE PARK IN THE TALKBOX.MOM SUBSCRIPTION

USE JAPANESE AT HOME

T

learn it!

♥ ☑ *Got it!*

		the table	**テーブル**
			teeburu
♡ ☐	Go to the table.	テーブルのところに行って。
			Teeburuno tokoroni itte.
♡ ☐	It's time to eat.	食べる時間だよ。
			Taberu jikandayo.
♡ ☐	Set the table.	テーブルをセットして。
			Teeburuwo setto shite.
♡ ☐	Sit at the table. (*Take a seat.*)	席について。
			Sekini tsuite.

> LANGUAGE GUIDES FOR SETTING THE TABLE AND DINING IN THE TALKBOX.MOM SUBSCRIPTION

USE JAPANESE AT HOME

T

- ♥ ☑ Let's color at the table. — テーブルで塗り絵しようね。
  Teeburude nurie shiyoune.
- ♡ ☐ He/She is hiding under the table. — (Name)はテーブルの下に隠れてるよ。
  (Name)wa teeburuno shitani kakureteruyo.
- ♡ ☐ Take turns. — 順番ね。
  Junbanne.

to talk 話す
hanasu

- ♡ ☐ Come talk to me. — こっちに来てお話しして。
  Kocchini kite ohanashi shite.
- ♡ ☐ I need to talk to you. — お話がある。
  Ohanashiga aru.
- ♡ ☐ Your mom wants to talk to you. — ママがお話したいって。
  Mamaga ohanashi shitaitte.
- ♡ ☐ Your dad wants to talk to you. — パパがお話したいって。
  Papaga ohanashi shitaitte.
- ♡ ☐ What are you talking about? — 何の話？
  Nanno hanashi?
- ♡ ☐ Shhh. Don't talk so loud. — しー。そんなに大きな声で話さないで。
  Shii. Sonnani ookina koede hanasanaide.

T

	What do you want to talk about?	何の話がしたいの? Nanno hanashiga shitaino?

the tape テープ
teepu

	Here's a piece of tape.	はい、セロテープ。 Hai, seroteepu.
	Can you tape the paper?	紙をテープでとめられる? Kamiwo teepude tomerareru?
	Can you tape the box shut?	箱のふたをテープでとめてくれる? Hakono futawo teepude tomete kureru?

to taste 味わう
ajiwau

	Taste the soup.	スープ味見してみて。 Suupu ajimi shitemite.
	The food tastes so good.	すごく美味しい。 Sugoku oishii.
	The juice tastes bad.	このジュース美味しくない。 Kono juusu oishiku nai.
	It tastes like strawberries.	イチゴみたいな味がする。 Ichigo mitaina ajiga suru.

USE JAPANESE AT HOME

T

♥ ☑
♡ ☐ **Thank you.** ありがとう
Arigatou.

♡ ☐ Thank you so much! どうもありがとう！
Doumo arigatou!

thirsty のどが渇く
nodoga kawaku

♡ ☐ I'm thirsty! のど渇いた！
Nodo kawaita!

♡ ☐ Are you thirsty? のど渇いた？
Nodo kawaita?

> LANGUAGE GUIDE FOR DRINKS AND SPILLING DRINKS IN THE TALKBOX.MOM SUBSCRIPTION

to throw away 捨てる
suteru

♡ ☐ Throw away your trash. ゴミ捨てて。
Gomi sutete.

♡ ☐ Throw away your wrapper. 包み紙捨てて。
Tsutsumigami sutete.

T

to tie 結ぶ
musubu

I can tie that rope for you. ロープ結んであげるね。
Roopu musunde agerune.

Can you tie this? これ結べる？
Kore musuberu?

Would you tie my dress please? ワンピースのリボン結んでくれる？
Wanpiisuno ribon musunde kureru?

Tie your shoes. 靴の紐結んで。
Kutsuno himo musunde.

It's time to… …する時間
…suru jikan

It's time to wake up. 起きる時間だよ。
Okiru jikandayo.

It's time to get dressed. 着替える時間だよ。
Kigaeru jikandayo.

It's time to brush teeth. 歯を磨く時間だよ。
Hawo migaku jikandayo.

It's time to eat breakfast. 朝ごはんの時間だよ。
Asagohanno jikandayo.

It's time to clean up. お片づけの時間だよ。
Okatazukeno jikandayo.

T

♥ ☑		
♡ ☐	It's time to go to school.	学校に行く時間だよ。 Gakkouni iku jikandayo.
♡ ☐	It's time to go home.	家に帰る時間だよ。 Ieni kaeru jikandayo.
♡ ☐	It's time to go.	行く時間だよ。 Iku jikandayo.
♡ ☐	It's time for lunch.	お昼の時間だよ。 Ohiruno jikandayo.
♡ ☐	It's time for dinner.	夕飯の時間だよ。 Yuuhanno jikandayo.
♡ ☐	It's time to go to bed.	おふとんに入る時間だよ。 Ofutonni hairu jikandayo.
♡ ☐	It's time to go to sleep.	寝る時間だよ。 Neru jikandayo.

> LANGUAGE GUIDE FOR SCHEDULING YOUR DAY AND TELLING TIME IN THE TALKBOX.MOM SUBSCRIPTION

	the tissue	ティッシュ **tisshu**
♡ ☐	Do you need a tissue?	ティッシュいる？ Tisshu iru?
♡ ☐	Here's a tissue.	ティッシュ、どうぞ。 Tisshu douzo.

T

Please use a tissue. ティッシュ使って。
Tisshu tsukatte.

Throw your tissue in the trash. 使ったティッシュはゴミ箱に捨てて。
Tsukatta tisshuwa gomibakoni sutete.

We are out of tissues. ティッシュ切らしてるんだ。
Tisshu kirashiterunda.

I don't have a tissue. ティッシュ、持ってない。
Tisshu mottenai.

together 一緒に
isshoni

Let's play together. 一緒に遊ぼう。
Isshoni asobou.

Stay together. 一緒にいてね。
Isshoni itene.

You may play in the backyard together. お庭で一緒に遊んでいいよ。
Oniwade isshoni asonde iiyo.

T

the toilet / restroom トイレ
toire

the bathroom お手洗い
otearai

I need to use the restroom.	お手洗いに行きたい。 Otearaini ikitai.
I need to use the toilet/bathroom.	トイレに行きたい。 Toireni ikitai.
Where is the restroom?	お手洗いはどこですか？ Otearaiwa dokodesuka?
Where is the bathroom in your house?	このお家のトイレはどこ？ Kono ouchino toirewa doko?
Let's go to the restroom.	トイレ行こう。 Toire ikou.

the toy おもちゃ
omocha

Let's play with the toys.	おもちゃで遊ぼう。 Omochade asobou.
I got you a new toy.	新しいおもちゃ買ってきたよ。 Atarashii omocha katte kitayo.
We need to get rid of some toys.	おもちゃ、少し捨てないと。 Omocha sukoshi sutenaito.

T

♥☑		
♡☐	Ow! I stepped on a toy.	痛！おもちゃ踏んじゃったよ。 Ita! Omocha funjattayo.
♡☐	Put your toys away, please.	おもちゃ、片付けてください。 Omocha katazukete kudasai.

	the trash	ゴミ **gomi**
	the trash can	ゴミ箱 **gomibako**
♡☐	The trash can is full.	ゴミ箱がいっぱいだよ。 Gomibakoga ippaidayo.
♡☐	I need to take out the trash.	ゴミ出さなきゃ。 Gomi dasanakya.
♡☐	Please take out the trash.	ゴミ出してきて。 Gomi dashitekite.
♡☐	The trash can smells really bad.	ゴミ箱がすごく臭い。 Gomibakoga sugoku kusai.
♡☐	Throw... in the trash..	...をゴミ箱に捨てて。 ...wo gomibakoni sutete.

USE JAPANESE AT HOME

T

the tree 木
ki

Do you want to climb the tree? / その木に登りたい？ / Sono kini noboritai?

Look how tall the tree is! / 見て！大きな木だね！ / Mite! Ookina kidane!

ILLUSTRATED NATURE GUIDES + SCAVENGER HUNTS IN THE TALKBOX.MOM ACADEMY

to trip つまずく
tsumazuku

Careful. You might trip. / 気をつけて。つまずくよ。 / Kiwo tsukete. Tsumazukuyo.

Oh, no. You tripped. / あーあ、つまずいちゃった。 / Aaa, tsumazuichatta.

to try 試してみる
tameshitemiru

May I try your juice? / ジュース飲んでみてもいい？ / Juusu nonde mitemo ii?

Try on your new shirt. / 新しいシャツ着てみて。 / Atarashii shatsu kitemite.

T

Climb the tree. Give it a try. 木登りしよう。やってみて。
Kinobori shiyou. Yattemite.

All you can do is try. やってみるしかないよ。
Yattemirushika naiyo.

the TV テレビ
terebi

Do you want to watch TV? テレビ観たい？
Terebi mitai?

I like this TV show. このテレビ番組好きなんだ。
Kono terebi bangumi sukinanda.

You've watched enough TV. テレビは十分見たでしょ。
Terebiwa juubun mitadesho.

No TV today. 今日はテレビなし。
Kyouwa terebi nashi.

If you do that, you cannot watch TV. そんなことするなら、テレビはもう見れないよ。
Sonnakoto surunara terebiwa mou mirenaiyo.

What do you want to watch? 何観たい？
Nani mitai?

You can watch TV for twenty minutes. テレビは20分間だけね。
Terebiwa nijuppunkan dakene.

You can watch TV for one hour. テレビは1時間だけね。
Terebiwa ichijikan dakene.

USE JAPANESE AT HOME

T

♥ ☑
♡ ☐ You can watch TV for two hours. テレビは2時間だけね。
Terebiwa nijikan dakene.

♡ ☐ Turn off the TV. テレビ消して。
Terebi keshite.

U

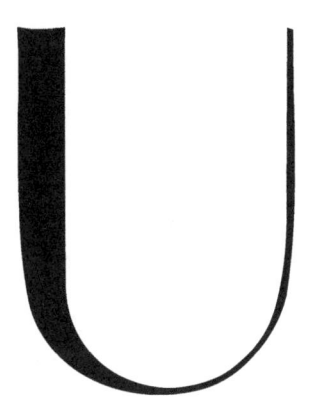

learn it!

♥ ☑ *Got it!*

		the umbrella	傘
			kasa
♡ ☐	We need an umbrella.	傘がいる。
		Kasaga iru.
♡ ☐	It's raining.	雨が降ってる。
		Amega futteru.
♡ ☐	Open your umbrella.	傘さして。
		Kasa sashite.
♡ ☐	Close your umbrella.	傘閉じて。
		Kasa tojite.
♡ ☐	Shake the water off your umbrella.	傘の水を切って。
		Kasano mizuwo kitte.

USE JAPANESE AT HOME

U

up 上
ue

The toy is up high. おもちゃがすごく高いところにある。
Omochaga sugoku takai tokoroni aru.

I can't reach it. 届かないよ。
Todokanaiyo.

Throw the ball up high. ボールを高く投げて。
Booruwo takaku nagete.

The plane flies up into the sky. 飛行機がお空に飛び立つよ。
Hikoukiga osorani tobitatsuyo.

Do you want me to pick you up? 抱っこして欲しい？
Dakko shite hoshii?

Pick me up! 抱っこして！
Dakko shite!

Pick me up from school, please. 学校に迎えにきてね。
Gakkouni mukaeni kitene.

upstairs 上
ue

I left my purse upstairs. カバンを上に忘れてきちゃった。
Kabanwo ueni wasurete kichatta.

I left my shoes upstairs. 靴を上に忘れてきちゃった。
Kutsuwo ueni wasurete kichatta.

U

❤️☑			
♡☐	I left my jacket upstairs.	上着を上に忘れてきちゃった。 Uwagiwo ueni wasurete kichatta.	
♡☐	I left my backpack upstairs.	リュックを上に忘れてきちゃった。 Ryukkuwo ueni wasurete kichatta.	
♡☐	I'm upstairs.	上にいるよ。 Ueni iruyo.	
♡☐	Go upstairs.	上に行って。 Ueni itte.	

> GET LABEL CARDS FOR ROOMS AND AREAS IN YOUR HOME IN THE TALKBOX.MOM SUBSCRIPTION

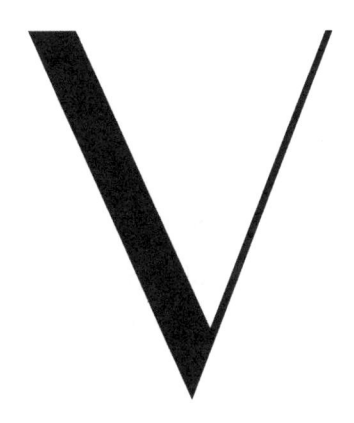

V

learn it!

♥ ☑ *Got it!*

	the vacuum	**掃除機** **soujiki**
♡ ☐	I need to vacuum.	掃除機かけなきゃ。 Soujiki kakenakya.
♡ ☐	Pick everything up off the floor.	床の上のもの片付けて。 Yukano ueno mono katazukete.
♡ ☐	The vacuum cleaner came unplugged.	掃除機のコンセントが抜けちゃった。 Soujikino konsentoga nukechatta.
♡ ☐	Please plug it back in.	コンセント挿し直して。 Konsento sashinaoshite.
♡ ☐	Are you scared of the vacuum cleaner?	掃除機が怖いの？ Soujikiga kowaino?

USE JAPANESE AT HOME

V

- He/She is scared of the vacuum.
  (Name)は掃除機が怖いの。
  (Name)wa soujikiga kowaino.

- Go in the other room.
  他の部屋に行ってて。
  Hokano heyani ittete.

- I'm going to vacuum.
  掃除機かけるよ。
  Soujiki kakeruyo.

- I can't hear you.
  何言ってるか聞こえないよ。
  Nani itteruka kikoenaiyo.

- The vacuum is too loud.
  掃除機の音がうるさい。
  Soujikino otoga urusai.

the video game テレビゲーム
terebi geemu

- Which video game do you want to play?
  どのテレビゲームやりたい？
  Dono terebi geemu yaritai?

- Let's play video games.
  テレビゲームしよう。
  Terebi geemu shiyou.

- Please turn off your video games.
  テレビゲームはおしまいにして。
  Terebi geemuwa oshimaini shite.

W

learn it!

♥ ☑ *Got it!*

	the wagon	ワゴン **wagon**
♡ ☐	Get in the wagon.	ワゴンに乗って。 Wagonni notte.
♡ ☐	I'll pull the wagon.	ワゴン、引っ張るよ。 Wagon hipparuyo.
♡ ☐	**Wait.**	待って。 **Matte.**
♡ ☐	Please wait for me.	待っててね。 Mattetene.

USE JAPANESE AT HOME

W

♥☑		Wait one second.	ちょっと待って。 Chotto matte.
♡☐		You need to wait five minutes.	5分待たないと。 Gofun matanaito.
♡☐		We've been waiting for five minutes.	5分間待ってるよ。 Gofunkan matteruyo.
♡☐		We've been waiting for ten minutes.	10分間待ってるよ。 Jippunkan matteruyo.
♡☐		We've been waiting for fifteen minutes.	15分間待ってるよ。 Juugofunkan matteruyo.
♡☐		We've been waiting for twenty minutes.	20分間待ってるよ。 Nijuppunkan matteruyo.

♡☐		**Wake up.**	起きて。 **Okite.**
♡☐		It's time to wake up.	起きる時間だよ。 Okiru jikandayo.
♡☐		It's not time to wake up yet.	まだ起きる時間じゃないよ。 Mada okiru jikanja naiyo.
♡☐		Please don't wake up your (*older*) brother.	お兄ちゃん起こさないで。 Oniichan okosanaide.
♡☐		Please don't wake up your (*younger*) brother.	弟起こさないで。 Otouto okosanaide.

W

♥ ☐	Please don't wake up your (*older*) sister.	お姉ちゃん起こさないで。 Oneechan okosanaide.
♥ ☐	Please don't wake up your (*younger*) sister.	妹起こさないで。 Imouto okosanaide.
♥ ☐	Please don't wake up your father.	お父さん起こさないで。 Otousan okosanaide.
♥ ☐	Please don't wake up your mother.	お母さん起こさないで。 Okaasan okosanaide.
♥ ☐	Please don't wake up the baby.	赤ちゃん、起こさないで。 Akachan okosanaide.
♥ ☐	Please don't wake me up.	私を起こさないで。 Watashiwo okosanaide.
♥ ☐	I need to take a nap.	お昼寝しなきゃ。 Ohirune shinakya.
♥ ☐	He/She woke up early from his nap.	お昼寝からはやく起きちゃった。 Ohirune kara hayaku okichatta.

to walk 歩く
aruku

♥ ☐	Let's go on a walk.	お散歩に行こう。 Osanponi ikou.
♥ ☐	Don't be lazy. Walk.	甘えちゃダメ。歩いて。 Amaecha dame. Aruite.

USE JAPANESE AT HOME

W

- ♥ ☑
- ♡ ☐ Is your baby walking yet? 赤ちゃん、もう歩けるの？
Akachan mou arukeruno?
- ♡ ☐ The baby can walk. 赤ちゃん、歩けるよ。
Akachan arukeruyo.
- ♡ ☐ The baby can't walk. 赤ちゃん、まだ歩けないよ。
Akachan mada arukenaiyo.

> GUIDES FOR WALKS, PLUS CHARTS FOR TALKING ABOUT WHAT YOU SEE, IN THE TALKBOX.MOM ACADEMY

to want 欲しい
hoshii

- ♡ ☐ Do you want that toy? あのおもちゃ欲しいの？
Ano omocha hoshiino?
- ♡ ☐ What do you want? 何が欲しいの？
Naniga hoshiino?
- ♡ ☐ I want a cookie. クッキーが欲しいの。
Kukkiiga hoshiino.
- ♡ ☐ I can't give you what you want if you are crying. 泣いてるなら、欲しいものあげられないよ。
Naiterunara hoshiimono agerarenaiyo.

W

to wash 洗う
arau

Wash your face.	顔を洗って。 Kaowo aratte.
Wash your hands.	手を洗って。 Tewo aratte.
Did you wash your hands?	手、洗った？ Te aratta?
Wash your hands again.	もう一回、手洗って。 Mouikkai te aratte.

> STEP BY STEP GUIDE FOR WASHING HANDS (THAT GOES ABOVE THE SINK) IN THE TALKBOX.MOM SUBSCRIPTION

to wash the dishes 皿を洗う
sarawo arau

Wash your plate(s) off, please.	お皿すすいでください。 Osara susuide kudasai.
Please wash the dishes.	お皿洗ってください。 Osara aratte kudasai.
I need to wash the dishes.	皿洗いしないと。 Sara arai shinaito.
I washed the dishes.	お皿洗ったよ。 Osara arattayo.

USE JAPANESE AT HOME

W

♥ ☑
♡ ☐ Help wash the dishes. お皿洗うの手伝って。
Osara arauno tetsudatte.

♡ ☐ Help me wash the dishes please. 私がお皿洗うの手伝って。
Watashiga osara arauno tetsudatte.

the watch うで時計
udedokei

the clock 時計
(often used to refer to a wrist watch) **tokei**

♡ ☐ Where is my watch? *(for a female)* 私の時計、どこ？
Watashino tokei doko?

♡ ☐ *(for a male)* ぼくの時計、どこ？
Bokuno tokei doko?

♡ ☐ Where did you put my watch? *(for a female)* 私の時計どこに置いた？
Watashino tokei dokoni oita?

♡ ☐ *(for a male)* ぼくの時計どこに置いた？
Bokuno tokei dokoni oita?

♡ ☐ Do you want to play with my watch? 時計で遊びたい？
Tokeide asobitai?

GUIDES FOR TELLING TIME TO SCHEDULE AND ARRIVE AT ACTIVITIES IN THE TALKBOX.MOM SUBSCRIPTION

W

to watch みる
miru

You may watch TV now.	今テレビ見てもいいよ。 Ima terebi mitemo iiyo.
What are you watching?	なに見てるの？ Nani miteruno?
A show.	テレビ番組だよ。 Terebi bangumidayo.
A movie.	映画だよ。 Eigadayo.
I'm watching you.	ちゃんと見てるからね。 Chanto miterukarane.
Will you watch the kids tonight?	今晩子どもたちのこと見ててくれる？ Konban kodomotachino koto mitete kureru?
I'll watch the kids while you run errands.	用事済ませてる間、子どもたちのこと見てるよ。 Youji sumaseteru aida kodomotachino koto miteruyo.

the water 水
mizu

Do you want some water?	お水飲みたい？ Omizu nomitai?

USE JAPANESE AT HOME

W

- Look at the water! / あの水見て！ / Ano mizu mite!
- Don't go in the water. / お水に入っちゃダメだよ。 / Omizuni haiccha damedayo.
- Don't step in the water. / お水の中に足入れちゃダメだよ。 / Omizuno nakani ashi irecha damedayo.

LANGUAGE GUIDE FOR DESCRIBING & DRESSING FOR THE WEATHER IN THE TALKBOX.MOM SUBSCRIPTION

---

the weather / 天気 / **tenki**

- What's the weather today? / 今日の天気は？ / Kyouno tenkiwa?
- It's raining. / 雨が降ってる。 / Amega futteru.
- It's snowing. / 雪が降ってる。 / Yukiga futteru.
- It's hailing. / ヒョウが降ってる。 / Hyouga futteru.
- It's sunny. / 晴れだね。 / Haredane.
- It's cloudy. / 曇りだね。 / Kumoridane.

W

There's a storm.	嵐だね。	Arashidane.

Welcome!	**いらっしゃい!**	**Irasshai!**
Welcome to our house.	我が家へようこそ。	Wagayae youkoso.
Welcome home!	おかえり!	Okaeri!
Thank you!	ありがとう!	Arigatou!
You're welcome.	どういたしまして。	Douitashimashite.

wet	**濡れている**	**nureteiru**
Why is the floor all wet?	なんで床がびしょびしょなの?	Nande yukaga bishobishonano?
Why is your bottom wet?	なんでズボンが濡れてるの?	Nande zubonga nureteruno?

USE JAPANESE AT HOME

W

Why are his/her pants wet?
なんで (name)のズボン、濡れてるの？
Nande (name)no zubon nureteruno?

the wheel 車輪
sharin

Your bike has two wheels.
(Name)の自転車には、車輪が2つあるね。
(Name)no jitenshaniwa sharinga futatsu arune.

Your bike has three wheels.
(Name)の自転車には、車輪が3つあるね。
(Name)no jitenshaniwa sharinga mittsu arune.

Your bike has four wheels.
(Name)の自転車には、車輪が4つあるね。
(Name)no jitenshaniwa sharinga yottsu arune.

He/She rides a bike with training wheels.
(Name)は補助輪付き自転車に乗ってる。
(Name)wa hojorin-tsuki jitenshani notteru.

He/She rides a bike without training wheels.
(Name)は補助輪なし自転車に乗ってる。
(Name)wa hojorin-nashi jitenshani notteru.

W

What? / Yes? 何?
(As in, "What did you say?") **Nani?**

to whisper 小さい声で話す
chiisai koede hanasu

Will you please whisper? 小さな声で話してくれる?
Chiisana koede hanashitekureru?

Please whisper. 小さな声で話してね。
Chiisana koede hanashitene.

What are you whispering about? 何、小さな声で話してるの?
Nani chiisana koede hanashiteruno?

to win 勝つ
katsu

I'm going to win! 私が勝つ!
(for a female) Watashiga katsu!

(for a male) ぼくが勝つ!
Bokuga katsu!

I won! 勝った!
Katta!

W

- [x] Let your (*older*) sister win this time.
今度はお姉ちゃんに勝たせてあげて。
Kondowa oneechanni katasete agete.

- [ ] Let your (*younger*) sister win this time.
今度は妹に勝たせてあげて。
Kondowa imoutoni katasete agete.

- [ ] Let your (*older*) brother win this time.
今度はお兄ちゃんに勝たせてあげて。
Kondowa oniichanni katasete agete.

- [ ] Let your (*younger*) brother win this time.
今度は弟に勝たせてあげて。
Kondowa otoutoni katasete agete.

the wind 風
kaze

- [ ] It's very windy.
風がすごく強いね。
Kazega sugoku tsuyoine.

- [ ] The wind is blowing.
風がビュービュー吹いてる。
Kazega byuubyuu fuiteru.

- [ ] That was the wind.
風だったね。
Kaze dattane.

W

to worry 心配する
shinpai suru

Don't worry about it. 心配しないでいいよ。
Shinpai shinaide iiyo.

I'm worried. 心配してる。
Shinpai shiteru.

I'm worried about... ...を心配してる。
...wo shinpai shiteru.

I'm worried about my test. テストのことを心配してる。
Tesutono kotowo shinpai shiteru.

Y

learn it!

♥ ☑ *Got it!*

the yard 庭
niwa

♡ ☐ Let's play in the yard. 庭で遊ぼう。
Niwade asobou.

♡ ☐ Go play in the yard. 庭で遊んできて。
Niwade asondekite.

to yell 大きな声を出す
ookina koewo dasu

♡ ☐ Don't yell in the house. 家の中で大きな声、出さないで。
Ieno nakade ookina koe dasanaide.

USE JAPANESE AT HOME

Y

♥ ☑
♡ ☐ Yell to your (*older*) brother to come in. お兄ちゃんに、お家の中に入って来てって、大きな声で言って。
Oniichanni ouchino nakani haitte kitette ookina koede itte.

♡ ☐ Yell to your (*younger*) brother to come in. 弟に、お家の中に入って来てって、大きな声で言って。
Otoutoni ouchino nakani haitte kitette ookina koede itte.

♡ ☐ Yell to your (*older*) sister to come in. お姉ちゃんに、お家の中に入って来てって、大きな声で言って。
Oneechanni ouchino nakani haitte kitette ookina koede itte.

♡ ☐ Yell to your (*younger*) sister to come in. 妹に、お家の中に入って来てって、大きな声で言って。
Imoutoni ouchino nakani haitte kitette ookina koede itte.

♡ ☐ **Yes.** はい。
Hai.

♡ ☐ Of course. もちろん。
Mochiron.

♡ ☐ Absolutely. 本当にその通り。
Hontouni sonotoori.

Z

learn it!

♥ ☑ *Got it!*

	the zipper	ファスナー **fasunaa**
♡ ☐	Zip up your zipper.	ファスナー閉めて。 Fasunaa shimete.
♡ ☐	Your fly is down. *(on your pants)*	ファスナー開いてるよ。 Fasunaa aiteruyo.

> GUIDE FOR FIXING COMMON DRESSING MISHAPS, LIKE UNZIPPED PANTS, IN THE TALKBOX.MOM SUBSCRIPTION

	the zoo	動物園 **doubutsuen**
♡ ☐	We're going to the zoo today.	今日は動物園に行くんだ。 Kyouwa doubutsuenni ikunda.

Helping Children Reply Back

"I want my child to use their phrases without prompting."

Then let's jump in and get one thing straight: the word "education" comes from the word "educe," which means to "bring out" or "draw forth."

It does not mean to pack in.

This means that goals like:

- ✖ memorizing a phrase
- ✖ perfect pronunciation
- ✖ learning everything at once
- ✖ remembering right away

aren't actually educational goals.

Notice how all of these "goals" focus on the result. These "goals" are focused on packing information into a child for them to perform perfectly. With closer examination, we see "wishes" masquerading as "goals."

Wishes are dreams that are outside of your control. For example, you can't control if your child memorizes something, and you can't control if your child's pronunciation is perfect. You can really, really want it, or even grumble, "I will *make* them do it!" But you cannot control it.

Goals on the other hand are dreams that are in your control. What's inside your control? The PROCESS that sets your child in the direction of the wish. This is 100% inside your control.

This means the way that you carry out your Practice Sessions changes everything. If you're skipping steps and nitpicking (aka focused on the results instead of the process), you're going to run into trouble.

Remember, "a horse that wants to race will always beat a horse that is forced."

I see this over and over again. Parents who focus on the process pass up the trajectory of what they previously planned to achieve. Whereas parents who focus on the results carry a level of anxiety with them that increases as the disparity between the wish and reality increases over time. This anxiety weighs on the child or comes out in outbursts from the parent, creating a teary-eyed mess.

Learning to use a language with your family should be a place of connection and joy. It should be an endearing memory. So if you've made Japanese a chore instead of a pleasure, it's time to reset and refocus. It's not too late. You'll be able to create healing experiences as you focus on a true education.

There are four very effective ways to educate or draw forth:

- ☑ Inspiring
- ☑ Enticing
- ☑ Loving
- ☑ Rewarding

Note bribing is giving someone something to stop bad behavior. Rewarding is having a clearly stated reward and working towards that reward to encourage good behavior.

Your goal as you create an immersion environment in your

home is to help draw forth the desire for your child to use the language. For some parents, this can be a piece of cake with their child. For those same parents, it can be a whole different story with another one of their kids.

With that said, you are the best, most invested person to help your child. As you read through the ideas in each of these categories below, I want you to try the ones that you think will speak to your child or, at least, be inspired by these. And if you fail, fail fast and try again.

Inspiring - *create a positive feeling in a person*

- Model practicing and using the phrases yourself with excitement and enthusiasm.
- Give your child a sense of control: Do you want to practice this phrase or this phrase? You're in charge of playing the audio. You're in charge of assigning emotions.
- Share the new phrases you've learned with trusted family and friends, proudly showcasing your skills.
- Change your scenery to somewhere you don't typically practice.

Enticing - *attract or tempt by offering pleasure or advantage*

- If your child asks for a favorite snack nicely in the foreign language, happily give it to them.
- If your child asks for your service nicely in the foreign language, serve your child.
- Make your Practice Session fun with your child's interests in mind.
- Eat food or dessert from the country as you practice or serve a favorite drink.

- Put the language guides at your child's eye level.

Loving - *consider how your child feels loved*

- Words of affirmation: Use effective praise that focuses on the process—not the result.
- Quality time: Have a special Practice Session or review time with one child.
- Physical touch: Snuggle as you practice. High-five or hug after trying a phrase.
- Acts of service: After practicing, surprise your child by cleaning something for them, solving a problem for them, or making a snack for them.
- Receiving gifts: A special present to practice phrases in a new box or challenge.

Rewarding - *choose a reward and work towards it*

- A movie night out together or a fun restaurant after completing 10 Practice Sessions.
- Extra video game time, time with friends, or other activity time per Practice Session.
- A trip with one child or the whole family to a country that speaks the language.

As you work through the TalkBox.Mom Program, you'll notice that our program revolves around true educational goals and not wishes. This is why our families succeed, and you can too!

Getting Outside your Comfort Zone

Don't fall into the trap that your Japanese needs to be at a certain level to talk with other Japanese speakers. Quite the opposite. You should definitely take advantage of solid opportunities to practice what you can say and learn from others as you talk. These experiences will stretch you, helping you to continue to grow.

However, these humbling experiences can feel extremely frightening. In the face of **speaking** *to get better at* **speaking** *another language*, many language learners retreat and engage in shadow activities.

Shadow activities, as coined by Stephen Pressfield, are activities that lie in the shadow of your goal. These activities seem like you're working toward your goal, but you're actually avoiding what will really help you to improve.

Notice above that I wrote "speaking" to get better at "speaking." Shadow activities would be doing everything but "speaking" to get better at "speaking." Like, memorizing vocabulary words, writing, doing grammar activities, and reading.

These activities will help you get better at *those* activities, but they won't push you further towards your goal of **speaking** another language like actually **speaking** another language will.

And when you improve your ability to speak, you fast track your vocabulary growth as well as your ability to gain fluency in reading, writing, and grammar.

Wait. Why is that? Let's take a look at the Fluency Pyramid and years of research.

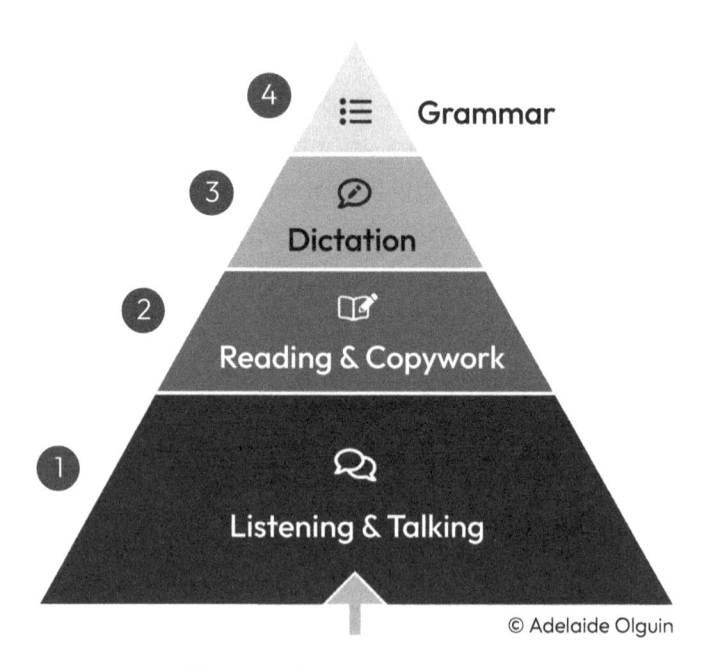

Fluency Pyramid:
- 4. Grammar
- 3. Dictation
- 2. Reading & Copywork
- 1. Listening & Talking

© Adelaide Olguin

**First and most important:
The foundation for fluency.**

The foundation of fluency is Listening & Talking. Research shows that children need to hear over 46 million words by the age of four to prepare them for school.[9] To create a foundation for reading, a child needs to have clocked 20,000 hours of listening through infancy and early childhood. [10]

This means that just because your child can read in English, it does not mean that it's time for them to read to themselves in Japanese. You're disregarding all the work you did as a parent in the Listening & Talking Layer for your child's first language.

What happens if you skip ahead? You slow down fluency or never reach it. For example, if your child is reading a word in Japanese, that word should create an image or meaning in their head. The reference for this word comes from their experience of using the word in a phrase.

If your child has to translate the word from Japanese to English, this is NOT fluency. They're translating. Therefore, you want to create a strong foundation of listening and talking before you move on to other fluency layers.

As you spend a couple of years building out the Listening and Talking layer, your child's ability to read in Japanese will develop much faster. Then as you read and do copywork, your child's ability to do transcription will develop even faster. And if you choose next to work on formal grammar, your child will already have such a trained ear and eye for grammar that they won't lack context to quickly understand grammar principles that they already use naturally.

Notice how all the fluency layer's build on each other. This follows the natural progression found in learning a first language.

One comment that I hear as I explain fluency layers is that in English you don't know every word and you look words up in the dictionary. Exactly. You're looking up the word in English and the description in English is giving meaning to the word. A great time to start reading in Japanese is when you can look up words in a Japanese dictionary and understand their meaning from the description in Japanese.

Now that you understand how important laying the foundation for the Listening & Talking Fluency Layer is... it doesn't make it any less scary! You might feel the same pull to shadow activities because they are in your comfort zone.

I would love to assign you some Fluency Layer Activities to help gently push you outside your comfort zone while you don't lose track of where your focus should be.

Fluency Layer Activities are immersion experiences that are supported by the core of the Fluency Layer. For example, the core of Listening & Talking is your Phrase Practice Sessions and using your phrases.

Some of the Fluency Layer Activities are: watching TV shows, movies, or YouTube videos, listening to music and podcasts, and, most importantly, talking to native speakers.

Do note that watching and listening to media will become shadow activities if you are not actively building out the core of Listening & Talking by practicing and using your phrases together. Likewise, you'll enjoy an accelerated progress as you talk with native speakers outside your home if you're in turn practicing and using your phrases with your family.

Here are some steps that we go into more detail in the TalkBox.Mom Signature Program that will gently help you step outside your comfort zone and grow.

First, when listening to media in Japanese or other Japanese speakers, listen for the words you do know. Second, feel really good about everything you DO know. Your ability to hear separate words in sentences even if you don't know what each word means is a big step.

Next, realize that it's okay not to know every word. You don't have to understand everything to get an idea of what is happening. From body language and tone, you can make educated guesses, which is what many foreigners do.

The last step can be the hardest, but, of course, it's the most important. You need to let people know that you don't understand a critical word. Ask what it means. If you can, add a note in your phone or notebook with new words or phrases you hear from other people. Most people love to help!

Likewise, if you hear a critical word repeated in any form of media you're listening to or watching in Japanese, write that word down and then look it up later. You'll get burnt out fast if you write down everything, so really focus on words you hear repeated often.

As you step outside your comfort zone, remind yourself and your family that welcoming what you don't know instead of fearing it will help you learn faster and become more comfortable speaking Japanese.

I've filled the next section, Your Toolbox, with phrases you can use when you are in these situations or are helping your child to say new words. I'm excited for you to slowly move outside your comfort zone—inch by inch—and look back at your progress in amazement.

Your Toolbox

♥ ☑ *learn it!* *Got it!*

- ♡ ☐ **Say...** — ...って言って。
  ...tte itte.
- ♡ ☐ **Repeat after me.** — 後に繰り返して。
  Atoni kurikaeshite.
- ♡ ☐ **How do you say this word?** — この言葉、なんて言うの？
  Kono kotoba nante iuno?
- ♡ ☐ **How do you pronounce this word?** — この言葉、どう発音するの？
  Kono kotoba dou hatsuon suruno?
- ♡ ☐ **What does this mean?** — これどういう意味？
  Kore douiu imi?
- ♡ ☐ **What does this word mean?** — この言葉、どういう意味？
  Kono kotoba douiu imi?
- ♡ ☐ **Do you know what this word means?** — この言葉の意味知ってる？
  Kono kotobano imi shitteru?
- ♡ ☐ **I don't know that word.** — その言葉は知らない。
  Sono kotobawa shiranai.
- ♡ ☐ **Let's look it up.** — 調べてみよう。
  Shirabete miyou.
- ♡ ☐ **I don't know what you said.** — なんて言ったかわからなかった。
  Nante ittaka wakaranakatta.

♥☑		
♡☐	Would you please say it again?	もう一回言ってくれませんか？ Mou ikkai itte kuremasenka?
♡☐	Would you please say it again slower?	もう一回ゆっくり言ってくれませんか？ Mou ikkai yukkuri itte kuremasenka?
♡☐	Please speak slower.	ゆっくり話してください。 Yukkuri hanashite kudasai.
♡☐	I just started speaking Japanese.	日本語の勉強を始めたばかりなの。 Nihongono benkyouwo hajimeta bakarinano.
♡☐	I learn Japanese by talking to my family.	家族に日本語で話して、日本語学んでるの。 Kazokuni nihongode hanashite nihongo mananderuno.
♡☐	I use a program from TalkBox.Mom.	TalkBox.momのプログラムを使ってるの。 TalkBox.Momno puroguramuwo tsukatteruno.

Goodbye

Can we not say goodbye?

♡   I'd love to meet you on the blog where I share resources, inspiration, motivation, and highlight families. Comments are definitely open to chat and ask questions.
www.talkbox.mom/blog

◉   Forget perfectly curated life and see how language learning actually looks at home and abroad. Come along with me as I help my kids speak other languages and as I help your family as well! Catch our team in our DMs.
www.instagram.com/talkboxmom

▶   Love longer-format trainings that you can listen to as you wash dishes, fold laundry, or go on a run? Subscribe to our YouTube channel to go deeper on creating a life that lights your whole family up.
www.youtube.com/talkboxmom

References

1. Mason, Charlotte M. (1925). *Home Education*, 301.
2. Mason, Charlotte M. (1925). *Home Education*, 306.
3. Mason, Charlotte M. (1925). *Home Education*, 157.
4. Mason, Charlotte M. (1925). *Home Education*, 301.
5. Mason, Charlotte M. (1925). *Home Education*, 80.
6. Mason, Charlotte M. (1925). *Home Education*, 80.
7. Mason, Charlotte M. (1925). *Home Education*, 80.
8. Mason, Charlotte M. (1925). *Home Education*, 301.
9. Hart B, Risley TR. (1999). The Social World of Children Learning to Talk.
10. Dehaene S. (2009). Reading in the Brain: The Science and Evolution of a Human Invention.

Index

A

absolutely 266
act 139
afraid 88
afternoon 137
again **37**, 68, 255
all better 214
all done **38**
all gone **39**
alone 226
already 48, 66, 69
another 123
answer 100, 149
arm 140
art 203
asleep 51
awake 95, 218
away 127

B

baby 51, 65, 85, 95, 99, 125, 147, 148, 170, 176, 187, 190, 200, 207, 218, 253
baby bag **41**, 42
baby gate **125**
babysitter **42**
back 51, 89, 140, 143, 179, 190
backpack 120, 173, 247
backyard **43**, 239
bad **44**, 219, 233, 241
bag 120
ball **44**, 45, 63, 200, 210, 246
balloon **46**
balloons 46
band-aid® **47**
baseball 223
basket **47**
basketball 223
bath 38, **48**
bathroom 94, 240
bathtub 59
batteries **48**
battery 49
beautiful 81, 119, 151, 191, 197
bed **49**, 50, 134, 146, 238
better 111
bib **52**
Bible **52**
big **52**, 177
bike 44, **53**, 54, 161, 179, 260
binky **54**, 106, 173
bird 157, 184
bite **54**, 55
black 80
blanket **56**, 103, 158
bleed 58
bless **56**
blocks **57**
blood **58**
blow **58**, 60, 67, 262
blow up 46
blue 80, 217
boat **59**
boogers **60**
book **60**, 61, 80, 104, 225
bother 225
bottle **62**, 179
bottom 217, 259
bowl 92
box **62**, 63, 77, 180
boy 53, 191
braid 133
breakfast 237
break, to break 47, **64**, 118
break, to take a break **65**
breastfeed **65**
bring 73
broccoli 134
broke 64
broom **66**
brother 55, 58, 97, 126, 178, 193, 207, 216, 225, 252, 266
brush 133, 237
brush hair, to bursh

teeth **66**
brush teeth, to brush teeth **67**
bubbles **67**
bucket **68**, 209
buckle 72, 205
bug 205
burn 219
burp **69**
bus **69**
busy 139
button 110
buy 49
bye **70**

C

calm **71**
camera **71**
candles 58
candy 152
can't 41, 47, 54, 119, 124, 206
car 43, 52, **72**, **73**, 100, 117, 136, 164
care 95
careful **74**, 98, 168, 242
carrots 100
carry **74**
car seat 181
cat 125, 184, 186
catch 45, 218
chair 64, 175

change 37, 88
child 167
chips 39
church 129
circle 204
class **75**, 203
clean **75**, 93, 94, 152, 237
clean up **76**, 166
climb 115, 242
close 63, 68, **77**, 99, 101, 245
clothes **78**, 108, 152, 153
cloud **79**, 217
cloudy 258
coconut 219
cold **79**, 212
color **80**, 232
comb, to comb 82
come **82**, 103
come back 152
computer **83**
cook **83**
cookie 254
cookies 156
cooking 76
cool **84**, 224
couch 46, 91, 97, 103, 173, 222, 226
cough 212
count **84**
counter 76
crackers 208
crash 136, 177

crayons 80
cream 144
crib 180
cross 226
cry **85**, 254
cup 93
cupboard **77**, 180
cut 203, 204
cute 191

D

dad, daddy 95, 104, 113, 138, 232
dancer 87
dance, to dance **87**
dangerous 189
dark 79, **88**
daughter 179
day 138
dead 49
dentist 129
diaper 37, **88**, 190
diaper bag **89**
diarrhea 213
dig **90**, 209
dinner 83, 94, 109, 238
dinosaur 104
dip 68
dirt **90**
dirty 94, 153
disgusting 168
dishwasher **92**, 93

do **94**
doctor 128
dog 104, 125, 157, 184, 185, 205, 219
doll 43, **95**, 101
don't 46, 47, 50, 51, 54, 55, 56, **96**, 99, 193
don't want 115
door 77, **101**, 180, 193
doorbell **102**
down 89, **102**, 229
downstairs **103**
drag 56
dragon 104
draw **104**
drawer 78, 180
dress 237
dress, to dress **105**
drink, to drink **106**
drool 187
drop **106**
drum **107**
dry 89
dryer **108**, 153
dry off 108
dry, to dry **108**
ducks 84
dustpan 66

E

earache 213
earbuds **135**
ear infection 213
eat 38, 60, 97, 103, 109, 119, 127, 131, 165, 225, 231
eight 85
elevator **110**
emotions **111**
empty 47
enough 171, 243
errand 129, 257
evening 137
everyone 73, 199
everything 41
excited 112
excuse 112
exercise **113**
eye 141, 213

F

face 69, 92, 108, 255
fall **115**, 154
family 104, 211
fantastic 129
fart **116**
fast **116**, 130, 191, 199
father 253
favorite **117**, 123, 169
feed 95, 185
feel 111
fell 81
fifteen 252
fight 96, 225
fill 68
find 41, 54, 56, 89, 159
fine 138
finish 38, 109, **118**, 152
first 124
fish 184
five 84, 111, 187, 252
fix **118**
flick 60
flip over 68
floor 66, 91, 111, 136, 168, 259
flower **119**
flu 212
fly 136
fold 153
follow 184
food 50, 58, **119**, 178
foot 141
forget 62, **120**
fork 93
fort 165
four 84, 111, 260
Friday 43
friend, friends 99, 103, 138, 156, 174
fruit **121**
full 88, 241
fun **121**
funny **122**, 152
futon **49**

G

game 83, **123**, 124
garage 53
gate **124**
gentle 96, **125**
gently 186
get in 50
get off 178
get out 51
girl 53, 191
give 44, 48, 62, **125**, 148
glasses 103
glue **126**
go 110, **127**
go down 183, 218
good 95, 138, 191, 219, 233
good job **129**, 192
grass 103
green 81, 130
grocery 128
gross 116
ground 56, 106, 223
grounded 83
grow **130**
grumpy 112
gym 113

H

hail 258
hair 66, 82, **133**
hamster 184
hand me 66
hands 159, 210, 215, 221, 255
handsome 191
hang up 78, 153
happen **134**
happy 112
hard 68, 138
hate **134**, 186
have 60, 121, 184
head 140
headache 212
headphones **135**
hear 64, **135**, 250
heart 204
heartburn 213
helicopter **136**
hello **137**
help 42, 83, 93, 105, 166, 187
her 48, 55, 126, 145, 190
here 42, 111
hide 63, 232
highchair 181
him 48, 55, 126, 145
his 190
history 203
hit 96, 225
hockey 223
hold 106
home 200, 238, 259
homework 120
hot 58, **137**
hour 65, 176
house 46, 76, 104, 121, 167, 224, 240, 259
how 279
hungry **139**
hurry **140**
hurt **140**, **141**, 189

I

ice cream 128
in 47
itch **143**

J

jacket 247
jar 180
juice 106, **145**, 222, 233, 242
jump 50, **146**, 192, 226

K

keep 101, 156
key **147**
kick 46, 98, 210
kid 43, 48, 51, 91, 138, 185, 257
kiss **148**
kitchen **148**, 215
knee 141

knife 208
knock 101
knock over 57
know 112, **149**, 207, 279

L

lake **151**
lap 217
later 70, **151**, 152
laugh **152**
laundry 78, **152**
lazy 253
leaf **154**
leave 47, 127, 136, 159, 224, 246
left 125
leg 140, 143
lice 213
lie, to lie 51, **154**
lights 155, 178
lights off **155**
lights on **155**
like 61, 87, **100**, 119, **156**
listen **157**, 170, 173, 203
little bit 126
lizard 185
load 92, 93
lock 97, 124
long 172
look 46, 71, 79, 119, 133, **157**, 163, 177, 189
lose, to lose **158**

lost 159
lotion **159**
loud **160**, 250
love 50, **161**, 202, 214
lunch 238

M

mad 112
magazine **163**
magic **164**
make 49, 57, 66, 68, 149, **164**, 165, 175
math 203
may not 49
me 105
mean 99
mean, to mean 279
medicine **165**
mess 66, 77, 98, 149, **166**
messy **167**
minute 187, 252
miss 45
missing 54, **167**
mom, mommy, mother 105, 113, 138, 148, 149, 232, 253
moon **168**
mop **168**
more 39, 54, 113, **169**, 201
morning 137
mouth 46, 49, 141, 210

move 108, 153
movie **169**, 257
music **170**, 203

N

nap **171**, 172, 253
naughty **172**
need 41, 47, 48, 49, 52, 65, 69, 77, 85, 113, 128, 171, **172**, 190, 238
nervous 112
never 175
new 240
next **173**, 216
nice 171, **174**, 207
nicely 97, 99
night 43, 50, 137, 139
nine 85
no 55, **174**
noise 135, **175**
nose 58, 59, 60, 141, 143
not 111
nothing 134, 158
now **176**
nurse 65, **176**

O

ocean **177**
o'clock 43
of course 266

off 52, 99, **177**
old **178**, 235
on 52, **179**
one 65, 84, 102, 110, 243
open 63, 97, 101, 124, **179**, 180, 192, 228, 245
out **180**
outlet 189
outside 46, 53, 88, 97, **181**, 202, 224

P

pack 41, 89
page 163
pants 260
paper 80, 81, 107, 127, 203, 233
park 129, 173, **183**
path **184**
pebble 199
pee 88, 172, 191
people 186
pet **184**, 186
phone 120, **186**, 189
pick 60
pick up 45, 78, **187**, 246, 249
picture 71, 81, 104, 117, 202
piece 124, 233
pillow **187**

pinch 96
pink 81
plane 136, 246
plant 130, **188**
plate 64, 76, 92, 215, 255
play 37, 43, 44, 46, 49, 51, 57, 67, 73, 83, 90, 91, 94, 97, 99, 101, 107, 119, 121, 123, 147, 151, 156, 202, 208, 211, 227, 239, 240, 256, 265
please 42, 105, 112, 118, 123, 126, 145, **188**, 261
plug in 188, 249
poke 98
pony tail 134
poop 88, 89, **189**, 191, 219
pop 67
post office 128
potty **190**
practice 223
praise **191**
present **192**
pretty 95
princess 104
puddle **192**
pull 101, **193**
pull out 89
pull up 68
purse 246
push 101, 110, **193**, 229

push down 110
push up 110
put 47, 49
put away 44, 54, 57, 74, 124, 153, 209, 241
put back 124
put down 45, 102
put in 63, 68
put on 63, 127, 205, 209, 227
put up 133

Q

quick **195**
quiet 99, **195**

R

rain 79, 197, 245, 258
rainbow 197
rat 184
rattle **197**
reach 246
read 52, 60, 61, 163, **198**, 225
ready 127, **198**, 219, 220
red 80, 81
restaurant 129
restroom **240**
ride 53
right this second 176
ring 102, 186

river **199**
rock **199**
rocks 68
roll, to roll 45, **200**
room 76, 77, 97, 120, 167, 172, 250
rope 237
rub 160
run 117, 223

S

same 111, 201
sand 90, **202**, 209
sandwich 54, 167
Saturday 43
say 120, 279
scared 112, 249
school 101, 128, 138, 161, 191, **202**, 211, 224, 238, 246
school bag 120
science 202
scissors **203**, 204
scratch 96, 144
scream 97, 225
seatbelt **205**
second 252
see **205**
seven 43, 84, 111
shade **206**
shake 198, 245
share **207**

sharp **208**
shirt 60, 91, 193, 201, 222, 242
shoe(s) 91, 202, **209**, 210, 237, 246
shore 177
shoulders 179
shovel **209**
show 94, **210**, 257
shut 233
sick **210**, 211
sing **214**
singer 215
sink **215**
sister 55, 59, 97, 166, 178, 193, 207, 216, 226, 253, 266
sit 52, 130, 190, 206, **216**
six 84, 111
sky **217**, 246
slam 99
sled **217**
sleep 51, 56, 95, **218**, 234, 238
slide 183, **218**
slippery 168
slow 199
slowly 99
smart 191
smell **219**
smile **220**
snack **220**
snake 185

sneeze **220**
snow 258
snowman 164
snuggle **221**
soap 153, **221**
soccer 223
sock 167
soft 68
something 154
son 179
song 214
sore throat 212
sorry 47, 120, **221**, 222
soup 233
spill **222**
spit 96, 225
spit up **222**
spoon 92
sports 192, **223**
square 204
stand 47, 73, 173, 174, 206
star **224**
start 93, 152, 153
stay 50, 111, 184, 206, 239
step 136, 189, 241
stick 107, **224**
sticker 224
still **225**
stinky 88
stomach 141, 189
stomachache 211

USE JAPANESE AT HOME   289

stop 51, 73, 140, 152, **225**
store 128
storm 259
story 50
strawberries 233
street **226**
stressed 112
stroller 180, **227**
strong 191, 227
stuffed animal **234**
sun **227**
sunblock **227**
sunlight **228**
sunny 258
sweaty 137
sweep 66
swim 151, 156, 223, **228**
swing 183, **229**

T

table 75, 77, 97, 157, 178, 208, **231**
tablet 189
take 44, 48, 59, 72, 74, 165
take off 63, 177, 205
take out 241
talk **232**, 233
tall 242
tangled 133
tap 107
tape **233**

taste **233**
teacher 156, 203
tease 226
teddy bear **234**
teeth 67, 237
tell 50, 154, **235**
ten 85, 252
terrible 138
test 202, 263
text, to text **235**
thank you 122, 235, **236**
think 42, 158
thirsty **236**
this 279
three 84, 110, 260
throat 212
throw 45, 200, 239
throw away **236**
throw up 212
tie 209, **237**
time 48, 50, 52, 62, 75, 76, 83, 112, 127, 165, 171, 173, 218, **237**, 238
tired 139
tissue 59, **238**
today 138, 190, 202
together 198, **239**
toilet 190, **240**
tomatoes 130
tomorrow 70
tonight 42, 168
too much 127

touch 98, 189, 208
toy 47, 48, 64, 77, 97, 106, 117, 118, 125, 158, 187, 206, **240**
toy box **62**
train 260
trampoline 146
trash 66, 236, **241**
trash can 66
treasure 90
tree 154, 157, **242**, 243
trip **242**
trouble 196, 203
truth 154
try 37, **242**
turn 48, 232
turn down 170
turn off 155, 170, 244, 250
turn on 155, 170
turn up 170
TV **243**
twenty 243, 252
two 65, 84, 110, 176, 244, 260

U

umbrella **245**
unbuckle 72
under 46
unload 93
unplug 189

untied 209
up 158, **246**
upstairs **246**

V

vacuum **249**, 250
vase 64
vegetable 131
video 37
video game **250**
voice 160

W

wagon **251**
wait **251**, 252
wake up 99, 237, **252**
walk 192, 204, 226, **253**
wall 81
wallet 107
wand 68
want 44, 47, 52, 67, 100, 102, 110, 121, 123, 145, **254**
wash 173, 215, 221, **255**
wash hands 38
washing machine 153
wash the dishes **255**
watch, the watch **256**
watch, to watch 37, 94, 169, 243, **257**
water 39, 62, 68, 99, 106, 119, 188, 222, 245, **257**
waves 177
wear 201, 205
weather **258**
week 211
welcome **259**
wet 50, **259**
what **261**
What 64
wheel **260**
where 41
Where 54, 56, 66, 73, 147
whisper **261**
white 81
Who 64
win **261**
wind **262**
window 64, 158, 228
windows 76
wipe 60, 92
wipes 42
wish 165
woke 139
word 279
work 68, 138
worry **263**
Worse 111
wrapper 236

Y

yard 53, 90, **265**
yell 225, **265**
yellow 80
yes **266**
yesterday 211
yucky 234
yummy 234

Z

zip 267
zipper **267**
zoo **267**